C000259874

BLACK WATCH

RED DAWN

The Hong Kong

Handover

to China

BLACK WATCH

RED DAWN

The Hong Kong Handover
to China

Neil & Jo Craig

BRASSEY'S

LONDON • WASHINGTON

Also from Brassey's

Barbarian Eye: Lord Napier in China
Priscilla Napier

Brassey's Companion to the British Army
Antony Makepeace-Warne

Churchill's Sacrifice of the Highland Division
Saul David

Copyright © 1998 Neil & Jo Craig

All Rights Reserved. No part of this publication may be
reproduced, stored in a retrieval system or transmitted in any
form or by any means; electronic, electrostatic, magnetic tape,
mechanical, photocopying, recording or otherwise, without
permission in writing from the publishers.

First English Edition 1998

UK editorial offices: Brassey's, 583 Fulham Road, London SW6 5BY
UK orders: Bailey Distribution Ltd, Unit 1, Learoyd Road, New Romney, Kent TN28 OXU

North American orders: Brassey's Inc., PO Box 960, Herndon, VA 20172

Neil & Jo Craig have asserted their moral right
to be identified as the authors of this work.

Library of Congress Cataloging in Publication Data available

British Library Cataloguing in Publication Data
A catalogue record for this book is available from the British Library

ISBN 1 85753 260 0

Typset by Hedgehog
Printed in Singapore

For Charles, Christopher and Sarah
with love and admiration

Tsing Ma Bridge. 27 April 1997
The opening of the Lantau Link to the new
Hong Kong International Airport at Chek Lap Kok.

(South China Morning Post)

CONTENTS

AUTHORS' NOTE

I spent my National Service, as a subaltern, with the 1st Battalion The Black Watch (Royal Highland Regiment) in Berlin, so my interest was ignited when I learned that the same battalion was to be the last garrison regiment in Hong Kong and to form the Army Guard of Honour at the final Handover Ceremony on 30 June 1997. As this seemed likely to prove not only a magnificent event but a savage test of its competence for any battalion, I decided I very much wanted to be there. Hence this book, which deals with The Black Watch and the Chinese People's Liberation Army as the principal, visible instruments of change, and with Hong Kong itself – that unique territory whose sovereignty both were sworn to uphold.

It is a personal record of some three months that my wife Jo and I spent in Hong Kong, two before the reunification with China and one afterwards, and it is a distillation of our experience and the views of the many people, from all walks of life, who were kind enough to talk to us.

It is not compiled from secondary sources – newspapers, magazines or second-hand opinions. We were not accredited in any way and, indeed, made a point of emphasising that we were not press and were working for ourselves. We also guaranteed anonymity for those who wished it and promised that there would be no recording during discussions. This explains the unattributed quotations. Though this had occasional drawbacks, on the whole it worked well, despite the necessity for many a silent dash to the nearest coffee-lounge for furious scribbling whilst memory held!

We tried hard to keep open minds; or rather, to keep reminding each other of our own prejudices and to listen and absorb. Of course, after 14 weeks right in the thick of it, we did form views – sometimes mild and sometimes strong – which we have sought to convey. We also worked at arriving in Hong Kong prepared, at least to the extent that a couple of non-Cantonese speaking non-Sinologists could, seeking advice and reading as widely as possible beforehand (see Bibliography) – especially about the People's Liberation Army and Deng Xiaoping's economic changes over the last decade of his life. Unsurprisingly, Hong Kong and its future is so complex that almost everything one writes usually needs instant modification.

As many photographs as possible are our own, but where we needed images from events that occurred before our arrival or that we were unable to attend, we had to rely on the kindness and expertise of others – which were always in plentiful supply.

Any project such as this requires much help and support in its different stages, and we have been very lucky in the generous backing we have received throughout. We are most grateful to Lord Wilson of Tillyorn (ex-Black Watch and ex-Governor of Hong Kong) and Major General B. H. Dutton CB. CBE (last Commander British Forces, Hong Kong) for talking to us and commenting on the book and that unique garrison.

During our gypsy period, we owe particular gratitude to the family – John Craig, Alex and Susan Catto and Harry and Angela Craig – for their immense generosity in accommodation, ideas and general support, which never wavered.

At the start, Andrew and Felicity Wedderburn gave warm encouragement and hospitality, as did Dermott and Trish Quinn, and Lt. Col. R. T. T. Gurdon (then Black Watch Regimental Secretary) reacted with enthusiasm and exhilarating speed. Lt. Col. S. J. Lindsay (the new Regimental Secretary) has carried on in the same vein. Dennis and

Audrey Freeborn gave much practical help and shelter, whilst Hilda Cannings was full of wisdom as well as finding a flat for us in West Sussex. Jean Nash was full of travellers' tales and good advice.

In Hong Kong, we are deeply indebted to Anthony Catto and Dafydd Angus for their offers of prolonged accommodation, which made it all feasible. Their local knowledge and constant advice were invaluable, as was Andrew Quinn's experience. Edward Stokes proved a mine of information on environmental matters and introduced us to the delights of the Shalotung valley and cold coffee.

All the people we contacted in Hong Kong were most constructive in their reactions, giving freely of their time and ideas, but we'd like to make especial mention of Alan Kemp, Iain Melville, James Ginns, the *South China Morning Post* – Grace Liu, Richard Cresswell, Patrick Carpenter, Ted Thomas, Tai Ming Cheung (China Analyst), Steven Strasser – Asia editor of *Newsweek*, Major Tim Craven – Queen's Gurkha Signals; and Ruth Vernon, Deputy Director, Joint Service Public Relations Staff. We thank Guy and Chujue Chambers for all their hospitality and help – plus memorable Dim Sum.

The 1st Battalion The Black Watch (RHR) in Fort George, Hong Kong and Edinburgh were unfailingly friendly and efficient and it is, in fact, invidious to pick out individuals. However, we record our particular gratitude to the Commanding Officer – Lt. Col. Alasdair Loudon; the Adjutant – Edward Jones; the Quartermaster – Jim Williamson; the Regimental Sergeant Major – Alan McEwen; the Pipe Major – Stephen Small and the Drum Major – Patrick McLinden for their ready help at such a hectic time. Lt. Col. David Price, Director of Music Scots Guards, generously made time to talk to us about the Band, rehearsals, the farewell parade, as well as providing photographs. Corporal Frank Proctor (the Black Watch photographer) shared his technical expertise and perceptive skills with great patience.

Win Win Photo and Processing Lab, Waterloo Road, Kowloon and Photo Scientific, Stanley Street, Central saw to all our photographic needs with friendly efficiency and humour.

On our return to the UK, James and Paula Loh came up with the perfect writing retreat and Emily Loh (and her agent) provided painlessly impeccable word processing. We are indebted to Sir Percy Cradock, Geordie Fergusson, Andro Linklater and Col. David Rose for permission to quote. Christopher Craig was our meticulous and imaginative editor.

We thank our agent, Adrian Hill, for his enthusiasm and advice throughout. Finally, we are grateful to Jenny Shaw and Brassey's (UK) Ltd for approving our idea and Warren Prentice, Caroline Bolton and Polly Willis for seeing it to completion.

Neil and Jo Craig
May 1998

BLACK WATCH

The night was pitch black. They hadn't expected it to be so dark or that there would be such a swell running. The launch wallowed from side to side as it moved out from the pier with its packed and silent cargo. The rain had eased off, but they were still soaking wet – they couldn't remember ever having been so wet – and water dripped steadily onto the deck at their feet. So far, things had gone well. Or had they? That storm was something else. Nobody had expected that. The sky above exploded in a huge star-shell burst of light, making them jump. After the dimness of the boat it was blinding. They felt adrenalin begin to flow again and excitement mount. After all it had been an evening they would never forget. They shook themselves and drew themselves up a little taller.

Now the night was ablaze with colour and sound – with explosions reverberating off the skyscrapers and rockets bursting like giant multicoloured clove balls. Triple and quadruple crashes hurtled over their heads towards the shoreline.

They became conscious of others stirring around them as they reacted to the excitement and the noise coming from a nearby ferry. There must be someone important passing because the passengers were all stamping, cheering and waving. 'Hey, they're cheering us,' someone shouted, disbelief in his voice. The applause grew; it was bedlam. They realised they were surrounded by scores of junks and other small vessels. They remembered the roar from the crowd as they had marched into the arena. That had given them a tremendous lift.

The launch stopped, wallowing. 'We're stuck,' someone said. It was the truth. In their enthusiasm, the milling craft had all crowded inwards and there was no way through. A tannoy burst into life. 'Do you need help?' The voice cut through the noise. 'Or have you decided to stay with us?' The Royal Hong Kong Police launch nudged its way alongside. 'Congratulations and thanks,' said the voice. 'Please follow me.' With a siren blast the Marine Police began to edge their way through the encircling crush.

Still the cheering and the stamping and the waving of hats in the air – it wasn't just Ex-pats, it was Chinese as well. It was Hong Kong saying goodbye. And all the time the massive fireworks were swirling, swooshing and crashing overhead.

Finally they were through and clear and reached Kai Tak pier. Their well-rehearsed moves clicked into gear.

2115 – 2135 hrs: Disembark.

2135 – 2225 hrs: Hand in weapons and change into civilian clothes.

Their white jackets were ruined. Better scrapped? Pack uniforms into suit carriers then suit carriers into boxes – all colour-coded. Then into the 'home' area where there was luxury packed food for them and cold fridges with a choice of six or seven cold drinks, tea and coffee. Finally they all began to relax.

2235 hrs: Arrive departure lounge. Board plane.

2350 hrs: Flight departs.

As midnight struck, they were taxiing towards the take-off runway – slightly behind schedule. Most yawned massively and stretching luxuriously in their seats looked at each other. Now they could really begin to party! They weren't to know that most would be slumped in exhausted sleep within the hour. Glasses were raised in silence, because the runway on which BA Flight RR01 was gathering speed for take-off had, some moments previously, become part of the People's Republic of China.

01 JUL '97 13:39 FROM COMMCEN EDINBURGH   TO 1 BW INVERNESS   P.01/01

Receiving Message

Storing Message
VZCZCCFA947   UU
OO RBDANF
DE RBDWC 4955 1821332
ZNR UUUUU
O R 011210Z JUL 97
FM MODUK
TO 1 BW INVERNESS
BT
UNCLAS
SIC ACA/Z3Q
FROM: HER MAJESTY QUEEN ELIZABETH THE QUEEN MOTHER
TO: LIEUTENANT COLONEL ALASDAIR LOUDON, COMMANDING OFFICER FIRST
    BATTALION BLACK WATCH
MESSAGE READS QUOTE
AS YOUR COLONEL IN CHIEF IT WAS WITH PRIDE THAT I WATCHED THE FIRST
BATTALION TAKE PART IN THE FAREWELL PARADE IN HONG KONG. YOUR
SMARTNESS, BEARING AND FORTITUDE IN SUCH TORRENTIAL RAIN DID CREDIT
TO YOUR REGIMENT, YOUR COUNTRY AND YOUR SOVEREIGN. I OFFER ALL
RANKS MY SINCERE CONGRATULATIONS.
                         SIGNED
              ELIZABETH R QUEEN MOTHER

BT

IMMEDIATE

COMMUNICATIONS CENTRE
01 JUL 1997
ARMY HEADQUARTERS
SCOTLAND

NNNN
End of Message 117 011338Z JUL

** TOTAL PAGE.01 **

Telegram sent by HM Queen Elizabeth the Queen Mother to The Black Watch after the Farewell Parade, 1 July 1997

CHAPTER 1

EVERYBODY CHEERING UP TO CELEBRATE REUNIFICATION

O n the morning of the last day of June 1997, wearing kilts, white spats and the distinctive red hackle of their regiment, soldiers of the Black Watch kept guard outside the open gates of Headquarters British Forces, Hong Kong. They checked documents as required and stood, mostly at ease (though watchful), responding amiably to the many enquiries from onlookers and looking directly at their cameras as they clicked.

Black Watch sentries, H.Q.B.F., Prince of Wales Barracks. (Craig)

On the morning of the first day of July 1997, wearing their No 1 olive-green uniforms, soldiers of the People's Liberation Army stood inside the same gates – still open but now barred – and guarded what had, overnight, become Chinese Military Headquarters, Hong Kong. They, too, checked documents as required but, at all other times, stood rigidly to attention. Smart, silent – and armed.

People's Liberation Army sentries, Prince of Wales Barracks. (Craig)

At midnight precisely, and half-way through the year, Britain had lost and China had regained, sovereignty over Hong Kong.

The soldiers of the 1st Battalion, The Black Watch (Royal Highland Regiment) and the People's Liberation Army were the visible instruments of sovereignty in Hong Kong. They had not met since 1952 when they had fought each other, on the Hook in Korea. Coming from very different historical traditions they symbolised, to the people of Hong Kong, two polarised ways of life – democratic and communist.

The soldiers of the Black Watch, like the rest of the British Army, hold a personal allegiance – they are soldiers of the Queen. Their Commander-in-Chief is, constitutionally, the Sovereign, and both she and her immediate heir are set above all considerations of political party. The government, too, is responsible to the Queen, and government ministers are ministers of the Crown. The soldiers of the People's Liberation Army hold not a personal but a political allegiance – to the Chinese Party-State. At handover time the then Commander-in-Chief, who was President of the Republic of China, was also Secretary-General of the Communist Party. The naval and air-forces, British and Chinese, played a part too but in the last weeks of British 'rule' it was the Black Watch whose presence was the more apparent in Hong Kong and the PLA soldiers whose imminence was the subject of so much anxious speculation.

Its future uncertain, the golden city became the centre of world attention and its people divided between their pride at the thought of being their own masters, and their fears that what they had so painstakingly built up might be taken away.

Amongst the aged, and not entirely secure, wielders of power in Beijing, the dawning of 1 July must have seemed a moment for which they could hardly wait, a triumphant event which, with a bit of luck, would cement their own positions. Nevertheless, one guesses that this excitement must have been laced with apprehension at what might be thrown up by the democratic elements – deemed by the Chinese leaders to be subversive – in Hong Kong society.

For millions of ordinary mainland Chinese, long targeted by the machinery of state-broadcast propaganda, the change-over was also cause for jubilation. And, because they had been left ignorant of the very different nature of the Hong Kong system, in their case the rejoicing was, generally, unalloyed. Millions of others, mainly peasants in the western countryside must have had little interest in anything that was going on in such a tiny and remote part of their huge nation.

Many educated Chinese, on the other hand, who well understood the realities of the situation, felt happy and patriotic, though quite aware of the dangers. Not just because they believed, or were at least optimistic, that what was happening to Hong Kong would be for the general good of China but also because they knew that, in all but the formality of official political structure, communism in the People's Republic of China was already in retreat and that closer ties with successful, capitalist Hong

Kong would strengthen the already burgeoning mainland capitalism – Socialism with Chinese characteristics – originated by Deng Xiaoping.

But whether or not people were interested or wanted to know, the Countdown Clock in Tiananmen Square in Beijing had, for two years, ticked away each second towards the arrival of what, officially at least, would be a blessed moment for all.

In mid-1997, Hong Kong was to be more than a paradise of fashion, jewellery and the latest technology. For a few days it became a showcase of sovereignty. The British, after a century and a half of political sway, were now on their way out but would not be seen leaving without a final flourish, a parade of troops on 30 June, to be watched by over 180 million viewers worldwide. This would be the last display of British rule in Asia, which would be replaced on 1 July by the Chinese with a show of their own, the cream of the three million men and women of the People's Liberation Army – the first stamp of their authority.

The Hong Kong police, too, had long been determined to give a performance with one eye on world consumption and the other, more sharply focused, on Beijing. They would demonstrate beyond doubt that they could handle Hong Kong's security without the help of the mainland Chinese.

The Bank of China Tower points gracefully upwards in the Hong Kong skyline, and mid-year, it too became the centre of more than usual activity, and the subject of ripe rumour and speculation. For example, it was whispered that the Chinese army now occupied top suites there from which, in any future emergency, it would command the new Special Administrative Region. There, weapons were already stacked, though forbidden to be used, or worn or even seen, before the opening day of Chinese sovereignty!

Near the present Bank of China lies the old and here, by way of a separate lift to the top, are the rooms of the China Club. From there, people said, after 1 July, Hong Kong would really be run, displacing the similar role of the nearby Hong Kong Club, the perch of Ex-pats, where critical manipulations had taken place under the British.

In Hong Kong, as the days passed, terminology altered, symptomatic it seemed of an alignment, or realignment, of public stance on the eve of the return to what was now increasingly referred to as the 'Motherland'. Announcements of special events became ever more joyful in tone. Advertisements of events to be held at Sha Tin Race Course under the auspices of the New Territorial Commercial and Industrial Association carried the slogan 'Angels spreading flowers to greet Hong Kong, everybody cheering up to celebrate reunification'. No ambiguity of intention here, even through the hazards of translation.

It was well known that the British Governor used to fill gaps in the schedules of visiting VIPs with a quick trip to the shops, and ordinary mortals, too, still enjoyed a spree, though things were getting more expensive.

In Hong Kong, jewellery is vivid and up front. As a Chinese acquaintance said, 'if you've got it, flaunt it', and 'we do like our rocks'. Big rings and big gems, thick watches – gold is best – and flashing necklaces. One dealer in watches and jewellery tut-tutted at a selected

Central District and Kowloon from the Peak.

(Craig)

5

MTR. Markings to help

passengers alight. (Craig)

model: 'That watch,' he said, waving a disparaging hand, 'is no good. Few, few dollar'. Then he pointed to one in solid gold, twice as large as the first and with strategic diamonds: 'This watch very good. Plenty, plenty dollar.'

Very few hats; umbrellas are far better. They are also *de rigeur* to deal with the heavy showers, and bare legs and flip-flops dry quickly. Walking pace is measured. The younger fashion in footwear is high platforms, which look heavy but are in fact very light and a great help through puddles, while the older taste is for delicate open shoes which let the rain water in – and out – and show almost universally beautiful feet.

In Central, the towering business district, people are always elegant, mainly dressed in cream, grey, black and white. Always black hair too, unless dyed for effect, as the Han Chinese – from the North – originally named themselves 'the black-haired people'. In hot weather, the Hong Kong Chinese wear cool, light clothes, and during rush hour in the Mass Transit Railway (MTR), the clusters of elegant commuters can be memorable; wherever you look you meet a pair of clear olive eyes with their calm Confucian gaze.

MTR stations are spacious and cool so that, even in the rush hour when the system is packed, somehow the crowds are unflustered and keep moving. Planned in conjunction with the police for maximum passenger safety, each MTR train consists of one long, articulated carriage without integral doors for ease of access and movement, and to discourage vandalism and violence. To date there has been no record of any violent crime on the service, although beneath each platform is a ledge for the temporary storage of suicides' bodies. On Sundays, squares, shaded pavements and fountain plazas are filled with gaily dressed Filipinas, who share exotic picnics, exchange goods, chatter, or go off to Mass.

Glitzy fashion shops are all around in Central and in Tsim Sha Tsui, at the southern tip of the Kowloon Peninsula, and in other parts of Hong Kong. In Pedder Street is Shanghai Tang, the store belonging to one of Hong Kong's richest entrepreneurs, David Tang; a fashion-house visited by the world's famous, evidence of which can be seen just inside the main entrance, on a wall display of familiar faces and trend-setters of all kinds.

David Tang's official poster girl is Gong Li, star of the East-meets-West film *Chinese Box*. His bright-coloured, Mandarin-collared Chinese-European line expresses his stated goal to 'act as a bridge' between diverse cultures, as he simultaneously fulfils the more typical Hong Kong occupation, the re-fuelling of an immense personal fortune.

(right) Window display, Shanghai Tang. (Craig)

Mandarin Oriental Hotel. (Craig)

Most restaurants have air-conditioning, and there is a wide range of specialised and national cuisine. Not much wine is sipped, especially in high humidity when the mouth is perpetually dry. Like coffee in the United States, tea is served automatically with any Chinese meal – wonderfully refreshing. Chinese waiters are reported to be ill-tempered because of the noise levels in which they work, but though Hong Kongers dining *en famille* can sound like the Battle of Waterloo, surly service is rare.

A lot of life in Hong Kong, especially for the poor, is lived in the streets. Stalls abound in narrow alley-ways, selling herbs, clothes, jewellery, electrical goods; there are open food shops with basic furniture and often no windows, where meals are cooked, almost on the pavement, with a lack of hygiene that can be hazardous for European stomachs. But there's a bustle and hustle that is irresistible and, to the outsider, there seems to be a higher level of contentment and cheerfulness than would be found in a British market. Or perhaps it is Chinese stoicism. One feels safer in the streets, too, because the crowds are friendly and a benign police presence is plainly visible.

Flowers are everywhere, sent with congratulatory messages to new businesses or temporary exhibitions, bouquets for both men and women at parties and weddings with ribbons in abundance – all presented with eye-catching Chinese flair. Local telephone calls in Hong Kong are free, and mobile phones are in constant use everywhere. A wrinkled old man pushes a heavily-laden barrow up a hill at Lan Kwai Fong. Bent almost double, he still chats animatedly on his mobile. Even in the first floor Gentlemen's at the Mandarin Oriental Hotel all is serenity until suddenly there is the well known bleep-bleep, followed swiftly by a barked conversation *in situ*. The attendant who hands out soap and towels looks put out.

A great deal of glass is used in construction work so that, for instance, there are wide harbour vistas from the Museum of Art, the City Hall and the Convention Centre; and comfortable seating from which to enjoy the views. There are also vast glass foyers with little streams and waterfalls as at Taikoo Place, Quarry Bay, where the *South China Morning*

Post has its offices. All are scrupulously clean and dotted with bookshops, clothes shops and coffee houses.

Banks, usually set on the first two floors of high towers, have armed guards, and distinguished solicitors have their prestigious offices above floors of computer, jewellery and camera shops. 'Photo Scientific' in Stanley Street, where films are developed, cameras bought and wisdom dispensed (free) about all matters photographic, is a favourite spot and is always buzzing.

In the China Bank, you have to change lifts to go beyond the 43rd floor. Going up and down in Hong Kong is as much the direction of travel as across and along. Levels of walkways are multiple, and there is a fortune to be made out of multi-layered maps. And, in the midst of the densely-packed skyscrapers, there are cleverly-wrought parks, often quite small with enchanting turns and twists, full of surprises, light and shade. There aren't masses of ebullient flowers – it is too hot for that – but hectares of leafy cooling green, with water. Hong Kong Park (the site of the original Victoria Barracks and of a memorial to Sergeant Major John Osborn who was awarded a posthumous Victoria Cross for his bravery during the battle of Hong Kong in 1941) is right in the middle of

Government House (left) from the China Bank Tower. (Craig)

Central, on a sloping-site and has fountains and cooling waterfalls – behind which you can walk – and deep pools with Koi Carp and Turtles that bask, like toothless geriatrics, on baking rocks.

There is an aviary, too – along the lines of the Snowdon model in London Zoo – which demonstrates a wonderful mixture of Chinese engineering skill and the delicacy of their design. You stroll through the cage on raised catwalks with periodic information stations where you can sit in sun or shade as birds fly over and under you and, sometimes, even around. Somehow you are made to forget you are behind a massive steel mesh edifice in the centre of 'busy-busy' Hong Kong.

And, of course, it being Hong Kong, everywhere the digger and the crane and the workmen with bamboo scaffolding, tearing down and rebuilding newer and better and higher, and reclaiming from the South China Sea. Hong Kong is constantly growing in girth as well as in height.

Hong Kong Park,
Central District.

(Craig)

Star Ferry arrival,

Central District. (Craig)

In Hong Kong spitting 'good riddance to the British' or feeling betrayed and deserted by them, or crying 'rape' and 'murder' at the mere thought of the arrival of troops from the Chinese People's Liberation Army were extreme examples of attitudes from a wide spectrum of reactions. Some, while glad to say farewell to British rule, still regarded it as the lesser evil, as the return to China seemed, at best, a step into the unknown. At least with the British you knew where you were. Yet others were respectful of the departing administration – for its efficient, uncorrupt Civil Service, the rule of law, free speech and, above all, its brilliantly successful economic system. Some of these believed that reunification with China would inevitably be the start of a quick decline in almost every aspect of life, though others believed the legacy was strong enough to be maintained. There were those – it is impossible to know how many – who feared that reunification would bring almost immediate Beijing control or even instant massacre at the hands of the incoming People's Liberation Army.

But the mood that pre-dominated, at least on the surface, was more moderate and pragmatic – the hallmark of the spirit of Hong Kong – sadness at the goodbyes, hope that things the things that mattered would stay much the same, regret that the best option of all, an independent Hong Kong run by the Hong Kong people, was not on offer.

Whatever emotions it aroused, the change of sovereignty was certainly unique in form: one nation losing, another gaining, with neither having won an argument or a war. Nor had the people of the territory themselves been consulted about the transition – the whole event stemming from treaties drawn up at least a hundred years earlier.

Arrangements for Hong Kong's future were agreed 13 years before the handover, in the Sino-British Joint Declaration of 1984 – giving plenty of time to set all in place or to get the jitters. Deng Xiaoping himself had declared a Beijing-controlled military presence, from 1 July 1997, within the new Special Administrative Region which, paradoxically, had also been promised 'a high degree of autonomy'.

Before June 1989, the most vexed question in Hong Kong centred on nationality and the rights possessed by those holding some form of British passport, to live and work in the United Kingdom. After the Tiananmen Square tragedy, this issue became red-hot, and the Governor, Sir David Wilson, flew to London to request UK right of abode for 3.5 million holders of Hong Kong British passports. His request was rejected by Prime Minister Thatcher though, in December 1989, British passports were provided for 50,000 Hong Kong households. This was intended to encourage key business and economic groups to remain in Hong Kong, knowing that, in emergency, they had a bolt-hole. The Chinese government responded to this move by inserting a provision into the Basic Law (the new Hong Kong Constitution) whereby no more than 20 per cent of the future Legislative Council could be foreign nationals.

To reflect Hong Kong's post-Tiananmen Square fears further, British negotiators tried raising the number of directly-elected councillors to the Legislature. Tightrope diplomacy resulted in the 1991 provision of 18 directly-elected seats, with a clear understanding of a slow but steady increase in such seats into the next century. On the British side, those who negotiated these terms believed that to have pushed for more would have been to endanger the whole undertaking – a prognosis later amply confirmed by events.

The decision to build a new airport at Chek Lap Kok (Lantau Island) was another attempt to restore Hong Kong's confidence in its own future. Beijing's approval was necessary, and China's suspicion that this was a conspiracy by the British to drain Hong Kong's coffers and thus devalue Beijing's 1997 inheritance, led the project into rough waters. Final agreement on the project was the result of skilful and protracted diplomatic activity.

Further signs of what Beijing considered subversive intention in Hong Kong – and a threat to the maintenance of order on the mainland – came with the 1991 election to the Legislative Council of Martin Lee, who was critical of Beijing power in Hong Kong after 1997 and, in 1992, the appointment and early performance of the new Governor, Chris Patten, who had replaced Sir David Wilson.

The adoption of Governor Patten's proposals for the Hong Kong elections in 1995 resulted in Beijing's setting up of the Provisional Legislature which ran parallel to the last period of British administration and met over the border in mainland Shenzhen. It would be followed, on 1 July 1997, by the dismissal of the existing Hong Kong Legislative Council and the swearing-in of the Provisional Legislature made up of men and women appointed (indirectly) by Beijing.

So, it was not to be the usual 20th Century progression from British colonial status to self-rule. Hong Kong under the British had not been called a colony but a 'territory' and once part of China it would become a 'Special Administrative Region'. This SAR was to be granted 'a high degree of autonomy' which was, in fact, quite a lot, though still not enough for many. It would keep its free-market, capitalist economy, its rule of law, its independent civil service and its free press. And, early on, it would have an elected legislature. But to many, the slightly ominous term 'a high degree of autonomy 'gave plenty of scope for anxiety, fear and bitterness both before and after 30 June.

Under Chinese sovereignty, the Chief Executive would be appointed by Beijing. Under British rule, the Hong Kongers had had no say in the appointment of the Governor, who was chosen in London but, whereas everyone knew where they were with the British and could count on 'fair play', no one could be equally confident about the Chinese. Would not the new Chief Executive be a mere Beijing puppet?

As with the British, under China the sovereign power would be responsible for both foreign and defence affairs. But Britain was far away and China was on the doorstep, and what seemed foreign in Beijing might be too close to home for Hong Kong. The British garrison had an on-the-spot Commander-in-Chief (who was also the Governor), but the People's Liberation Army would be under an ultimate authority sited in Beijing. And as to 'internal security', whose interpretation would prevail if there were doubt over whether a particular issue came under that heading or, more ominously, under 'national security'? The Hong Kong police were responsible, in normal circumstances, for internal security, but Beijing (and thus the PLA) for national security.

The Chief Executive first appointed was a businessman: an amiable, good man but nonetheless a businessman. China's financial investment in Hong Kong is huge and most of the richest men in Hong Kong were mainland Chinese and so, under the new regime, in whose interests would the city be run?

For the first year, at least, Hong Kong would have lost its elected legislature. Under British rule, this had only existed for a short time, but soon there would be just a Provisional Legislature chosen by 400 men and women, themselves selected in Beijing and not Hong Kong.

There were other considerations, too: anxiety about signs of self-censorship in leading sections of the Hong Kong press (criticism of the Chinese governing élite, for example, seemed to have ceased in the pages of the *South China Morning Post*); awareness of the high level of corruption within mainland business activity and fears of its poison infiltrating Hong Kong (with an obvious threat to international investment) and the challenge to Hong Kong's infrastructure from the threatened influx of thousands of mainland Chinese, including children who had 'right of abode' enshrined in the new Basic Law that was the legal bed-rock of the SAR.

These fears, then, and other problems and dangers perceived as inherent in the new regime gave rise to much debate, fear and occasionally hysteria during the weeks before and immediately after the handover, despite the often repeated assurances from Beijing that Hong Kong's 'high degree of autonomy' would be fully honoured.

In our conversations before and after the handover, people often brought up the vexed subject of the arrival of the main body of the PLA on 1 July. 'I'm sure they're not here to defend us,' and 'their arrival was like an invasion' were typical reactions. Others thought that any military person would understand the PLA's need to have a presence in Hong Kong before midnight on 30 June (an advance party had been sent in) and that regarding their entry as high profile was nonsense. Indeed, to many it seemed a low profile entry as it took place, well advertised beforehand, at 0600 hrs on 1 July, when the bulk of the population was asleep.

A retired British colonel, looking back at the handover period, told us that, in his view, the entry of the PLA had been 'not aggressive but normal'.

However, any attempt to understand Hong Kong's approach to the changeover of sovereignty to China must include the events of 4 June 1989 – Tiananmen Square – and the psychological scars that left. The anniversary of that tragedy had fallen less than a month before Reunification Day and all over the world images had flashed on television screens, reawakening past horrors. The same colonel who had assessed the PLA entry as perfectly acceptable, told us at the same meeting of 'those extraordinary Tiananmen pictures' which 'are still clearly in my mind'. And in 1997, those who had authorised troop action on that fateful day, or their immediate successors, were to become the ultimate masters of Hong Kong.

Other atrocities were remembered, too: scenes of the most brutal torture and butchery, committed in Hong Kong itself by invading Japanese troops in 1941 and during the years of occupation. Any wife of a young soldier killed in defence of Hong Kong – as many were – would now be in her seventies, any parent in their nineties, any child in their fifties – a high tide of remembrance, no less terrible and infinitely more prolonged than those seen in Beijing.

Thus for many, the prospect of the entry of large (though unspecified) numbers of troops coming again, as it happened, across the border from the North caused worry and alarm. For though they were Chinese troops this time, in many ways they came from a different culture, whose power-house in Beijing was the same power-house that had ordered the killing in Tiananmen Square. These fears did not come from overheated imaginations but from personal observation.

It was into this highly-charged political situation that the 1st Battalion, The Black Watch (RHR) had flown, in groups, during January and February 1997. These highly skilled, professional soldiers were not only to carry out the normal garrison duties that had evolved over the last 150 years but to prepare for and enact the physical handover to the PLA on 30 June, knowing the while that every man would be watched, every mistake noted and exposed – and occasionally over-exposed – by the press in the midst of one of the major political events of the 20th Century, with more media coverage than any event since the Gulf War. It would be six months in a goldfish bowl.

Engagement party at the China Club Old Bank of China Building. (Craig)

CHAPTER 2

HIGHLAND MEN WOULD HARDLY BE BROUGHT TO MARCH WITHOUT IT

Highland soldiers have fought with distinction on practically every battlefield of the British Army since William Pitt the Elder decided, after the 1745 rebellion which ended in the disaster of Culloden, to enlist these fierce turbulent hill men into the service of the Empire. The characteristics of these early Highland 'Jocks' were described by General David Stewart of Garth over 170 years ago. Of the clan spirit, he wrote:

> In forming his military character, the Highlander was not more favoured by nature than by the social system under which he lived. Nursed in poverty, he acquired a hardihood which enabled him to sustain severe privations. As the simplicity of his life gave vigour to his body, so it fortified his mind. Possessing a frame and constitution thus hardened, he was taught to consider courage as the most honourable virtue, cowardice the most disgraceful failing; to venerate and obey his Chief, and devote himself for his native country and clan; and thus prepared to be a soldier, he was ready to follow wherever honour and duty called him.

This is the seed-bed of the regimental spirit which is the cornerstone of the Black Watch, as of other good regiments. Sometimes criticised as fusty clinging to obsolete ideas, regimental tradition is, in fact, strictly utilitarian in maintaining cohesion, flexibility and morale. There is great

Black Watch Pipes and Drums and sword dance. (Frank Proctor)

strength to be found, when life is grim, in a history, a tune or a hackle.

Naturally, the Jocks have changed much down the years as has the nature of warfare. No longer the wild rush forwards with broadsword and dirk 'with a fury that would yield neither to discipline nor to death' but rather the fully motorised or airborne unit, skilled craftsmen with small-arms and communications, ready to operate even in a nuclear setting, constantly adjusting and training and preparing for future emergencies, whatever form they may take. As the Black Watch has always been.

However, they do seem to have inherited the spirit and traditions of their Highland forebears – the 'clan' feeling, the toughness, the fierceness in assault, the independence of character, the humour in adversity and the quiet self-confidence. They also still demonstrate the old ability to absorb anyone of whatever nationality or regiment that works with them. In India, for example, Tippoo Sahib marched against Mangalore on the west coast, whose garrison consisted of the 2nd Battalion Black Watch (500 men) with 1,500 Sepoys, all under Major John Campbell of the Highlanders. Tippoo Sahib hoped the size of his force would frighten them into quick surrender and was much put out when the Black Watch attacked his advance guard with a lightning sortie 12 miles from the city and captured all its guns. He then laid siege to the town and the walls were breached and reduced to ruins. There was daily hand-to-hand fighting in the rubble. But the garrison held out for nine months of slow starvation, eating their horses and dogs. Attempts to relieve them failed.

Eventually Tippoo offered honourable terms, the remaining Black Watch surrendered and marched out with flags flying and all the honours of war. And, so fond of the Sepoys fighting with them had they become, that they adopted 'these brave blacks' into their own regiment and renamed them the 3rd Battalion of the Royal Highland Regiment.

And nowadays anyone from the support forces, whether padre, doctor, accountant or engineer, who is seconded to the regiment is soon to be seen wearing a Black Watch bonnet with red hackle and exhibiting strange signs of going native. There is the archival story of a fierce argument between two Lancashire privates who found themselves in a Black Watch Battalion; it ended when one of them pronounced, with finality, 'Ah've bin a Jock longer than tha'.

Indeed, the memory of my own introduction to the Black Watch is still fresh. I was doubly nervous as I strode – shiny pips perched precariously on my shoulders – across the parade ground at Queen's Barracks, Perth (now no more) to report myself. Although when filling-in my call-up papers, I had specifically put the Black Watch as my first choice of regiment, the War Office in its infinite wisdom sent me to 68 Training Regt. RA. at Towyn, North Wales. At the end of our basic training, having passed my War Office Selection Board, I transferred – courtesy of a sympathetic Battery Commander – to Infantry Officer Training at Eaton Hall under the legendary Irish Guardsman RSM Lynch, famous for his dictum: 'Gentlemen! You will call me Sorr and I will call you Sorr. The difference is, gentlemen, that *you* will mean it!'

Towards the end of this period came the moment when officer cadets were told whether their choice of regiment had been accepted. The Black Watch representative – a rather languid captain who did not match up to my ideal of a Highland Officer – summoned me to his office and said, without looking up: 'Ah! Craig. You've been accepted by the Black Watch ... there must be some mistake ... I'll check. Dismiss.'

However, the Black Watch stuck to its original decision, which was why I was heading across the square at Queen's Barracks, with mixed feelings. The RQMS himself shook my hand, welcomed me to the regiment and handed me my kilt. 'There you are, Sir ... your kilt. The finest garment in the world for fornication and diarrhoea.'

I moved on to the Officers' Mess to see if any of the other new subalterns had arrived but it was empty except for one solitary figure reading a newspaper. He rose from his seat and turned, smiling: it was Brigadier Bernard Fergusson (as he was then). I had read his book *The Black Watch and the King's Enemies*, a history of the regiment during the Second World War. In his foreword to the book, Field Marshall Wavell had written of its author: 'As a soldier, he made a contribution to the war, in command and on the staff, which few of the younger generation equalled'.

He was a towering regimental figure. What an opportunity! So many questions to ask, so much to find out. I stood there, overcome, whilst he courteously bade me welcome, chatted easily about this and that, and then moved to the door. 'Must be off. You'll enjoy Berlin, Mr Craig, and having a platoon of your own. You're lucky. It's a great privilege and there really is no better command in the army. Take things slowly and be yourself. It's difficult for you national servicemen, I know, but you'll do well.' And the door closed behind him.

The ancestors of the Black Watch came on the scene in 1624. That was when the government started raising Independent Companies made up solely of Highlanders, to police their own countryside. Then, in 1667, King Charles II issued a commission under the Great Seal to the Earl of Atholl to raise as many men as he needed 'to be a constant guard for securing the peace of the Highlands' and 'to watch upon the braes'. These guards were supposed to prevent cattle thieving and the like and were also to stop blackmail, the original protection racket, by which the wild Highlanders got money from the better-off Lowland farmers.

These experiments in rural policing continued for the rest of the century but were not an unqualified success. At times the arms were misused and the loyalty of the Highlanders was not always unwavering. There was fiddling and corruption on the side because, instead of bringing criminals to justice, the Highland Watch often 'compounded for the theft, and for a sum of money set them at liberty'. One general of the period reported that they also defrauded the government by drawing pay for twice as many men as they had in arms.

Black Watch: anti-smuggling patrol boat.
1997. (Frank Proctor)

In 1719, because of the turmoil after the 1718 rebellion, King George I disbanded the Independent Companies. Highlanders were forbidden to carry arms and any clansman found with a claymore in his hand could be shipped overseas to serve in the English army. The hope was that the bearing of arms would die out through lack of use.

Then in 1724 General George Wade – who built the roads and bridges that led to the gradual 'civilisation' of the Highlands – was appointed Commander-in-Chief in Scotland. He re-formed six Independent Companies of Highlanders reckoned to be loyal to the government. They alone were allowed to carry weapons and their function, as before, was to police the Highlands and keep order amongst the warring clans. The 500 officers and men came from loyal Whig clans – three companies of Campbells, and one each of Grants, Munros and Frasers. These were his orders:

> To officers commanding Highland Companies – that pursuant to their beating order they proceed forthwith to raise their non-commissioned officers and soldiers, and no man to be listed under size of 5 foot 6 inches. That officers commanding companies take care to provide a plaid clothing and bonnet in the Highland dress for the non-commissioned officers and soldiers belonging to their companies, the plaid of each company to be as near as they can of the same sort or colour; that besides the plaid clothing, to be furnished every two years, each soldier is to receive from his captain a pair of brogues every six weeks, a pair of stockings every three months, a shirt and cravat every six months.

Gradually, the Black Watch tartan of the dark blue, black and green sett came to be generally used. It became recognised as the 'government' tartan and today is worn in one form or another all over the world.

The locals started calling these Independent Companies *Am Freiceadan Dubh* – the Black Watch: 'Black' from the tartan they wore and 'Watch' because they kept an eye on the Highlands. There are other versions, however; that the 'Black' stands not for the colour of the kilt but 'for the black Hanoverian hearts of the wearers'; or 'Black' from 'blackmail', which they were sworn to suppress. However , the Black Watch did not become the regiment's official title until 1922, although it was used as a local nick-name (often pejoratively?) right from the start.

As regards the red hackle, in 1763, the regiment were patrolling in North America. One day they were ambushed and only extricated themselves by pretending to retreat and, as the American Indians whooped in for the kill, turning swiftly and ambushing them in turn. 'Only the dread of being roasted alive kept the exhausted troops at their work,' noted a later commentator wryly, adding that the red hackle probably began life here, as the Highlanders used to decorate their bonnets with feathers à la Indian head-dress.

Young Highlanders queued up to enlist in the Independent Companies mainly because of the splendid status symbol of being allowed to carry weapons, while everyone else still had to remain unarmed. The Companies had their own pipers too, dressed in red Stewart or Royal tartan, because 'the Highland men would hardly be brought to march without it'. General Wade ordered them to enlist

Black Watch: training.

1997. (Frank Proctor)

drummers as well. He felt that the drum was a more martial instrument. An ancient story goes that an argument arose in one company between the piper and the drummer over who should hold the place of honour as right marker. It ended with the piper exclaiming: 'Ods wuds, Sir, and shall a little rascal that beats upon a sheepskin tak' the right hand of me that am a musician?'

In 1739, as war with Spain seemed likely, King George II ordered the Independent Highland Companies to be incorporated into a Regiment of Foot, 'the men to be natives of that country, and none other to be taken'. The first Colonel was 'Our Right Trusty and Right Well-Beloved Cousin, John, Earl of Craufurd and Lindsay'. He was, in fact, a Lowlander, probably chosen to avoid jealousy amongst the clans.

The first parade of The Highland Regiment, 850-strong, was held in a field by the River Tay near Aberfeldy, beside one of General Wade's bridges. The statue of an early private soldier, Farquar Shaw, the son of a Strathspey laird, stands at the spot today.

A private in the new regiment wore light buckled pumps or brogues, in which he could run through the heather, red and white chequered stockings fastened with a broad red garter at the knee, and a tartan belted 'plaid' (Gaelic for blanket) 12 yards long draped around his body like a toga, which acted as cloak, tent, blanket, groundsheet and umbrella. To put it on, you laid your ox-leather belt flat on the ground, placed the plaid across it, pleating it neatly and leaving a bit at each end unpleated. You then lay down carefully on top and fastened the belt around your waist by its silver buckle. The part of the plaid below the belt became the kilt when you stood up, the unpleated part being the 'flat' front. The upper part sagged down over the belt and was fastened to the left shoulder with a pin.

The sporran was made of badger, doe, otter, seal or deer skin with the hair outside. The original Highland soldier wore a scarlet waistcoat, a short scarlet jacket with buff facings and various fancy trimmings of white lace. He had a flat blue 'pancake' bonnet with a red border. He carried a musket, a broadsword with basket hilt and a bayonet. Highland pistols and a dirk were optional extras. Most carried dirks. Sergeants had lethal looking 7-foot Lochaber axes.

Unsurprisingly, questions were asked and still are. In the early days of the regiment, some Highlanders were shipwrecked and landed in France. An observant local reported: '*Il est très véridique qu'ils sont sans culotte dessous.* 'Bums the Word' shrieked a headline in Hong Kong when a naughty wind revealed the same truth.

' ... we had not one man over the rest.'

Very few regimental histories begin with a mutiny, but that is what happened with the Highland Regiment, though in a somewhat abnormal situation. In 1743 the regiment were summoned south and mustered at Perth for the long march to London. Because they genuinely believed they had enlisted for service in the Highlands only – as had been the case with the Independent Companies – the Highlanders were very unhappy about this move and were only partially satisfied with the assurance that they were just going south to be reviewed by King George himself and would then return home. In fact they were bound for Flanders and the War of Austrian Succession.

Feelings were not soothed when King George left for the continent on the very day the regiment reached London, without inspecting them. The English, however, were very enthusiastic. One newspaper said: 'They are certainly the finest regiment in the Service, being tall, well-made men and very stout'.

Meanwhile, visitors to the Highlanders' camps in the country villages of Highgate and Finchley spread gossip and undermining rumours. The regiment, they insisted, was to be sent to the West Indies, which was notorious – through fever and disease – as a graveyard for British soldiers. The Highlanders brooded. They grumbled that 'after being used as rods to scourge their own countrymen, they were to be thrown into the fire'.

On the King's birthday, 4 May, General Wade reviewed the troops on Finchley Common. One newspaper reported:

The Highlanders made a very handsome appearance, and went through their exercise and firing with the utmost exactness. The novelty of the sight drew together the greatest concourse of people ever seen on such an occasion.

After it was all over, some 200 disgruntled Highlanders decided to head for home. At midnight they stole stealthily out of camp, taking their arms and 14 rounds of ball-cartridge each. There was panic at the news. What desperate acts would these 'savage mountaineers' commit in the defenceless Home Counties? The English considered the Highlander to be 'a fierce and savage depredator, speaking a barbarous language and inhabiting a barren and gloomy region, which fear and prudence alike forbade all strangers to enter'. Orders were rushed to all officers commanding in northern districts, exhorting them to intercept the fugitives, a reward of 40 shillings per deserter being offered for capture.

The Highlanders were led by Corporal Samuel MacPherson with much skill and flair. They moved by night and lay low, in woodlands and strong defensive positions, during the day. They kept to the open country between the two great northern roads, continually zigzagging their line of march. The usual contradictory sightings puzzled the authorities for four days but then a gamekeeper spotted them in Lady Wood, a hill four miles from Oundle, and squadrons of cavalry were soon clattering to the area.

The deserters were well dug in and were determined to die to the last man if they did not get a pardon. But during the night, for some reason, they laid down their arms. They had behaved with such discipline throughout the retreat that public opinion now turned full circle from horror to admiration. But this did not help the mutineers. One hundred and thirty-nine of them were tried for mutiny and, with the fine disregard for the laws of the land displayed by courts-martial over the years, found guilty and condemned to be shot.

The evidence at the trial, which had to be interpreted from the Gaelic, shows the 'mutineers' had only the vaguest idea of what their 'mutiny' was all about. Indeed 79 of them could not speak a word of English. But they all thought that the government had treated them unforgivably by bringing them south from the Highlands.

Private George Grant:

I am neither a Whig nor Papist, but I will serve the king for all that. I am not afraid; I never saw the man I was afraid of. I will not be cheated, nor do anything by trick. I will not be transported to the plantations, like a thief and a rogue.

Private John Stewart:

I did not desert. I only wanted to go back to my own country because they abused me and said I was to be transported. I had no leader or commander; we had not one man over the rest. We were all determined not to be tricked. We will all fight the French and Spaniards, but will not go like rogues to the plantations. I am not a Presbyterian. No, nor a Catholic.

Corporal Samuel MacPherson, his brother Malcolm, and Private Farquar Shaw were shot on Tower Hill. A newspaper reported:

The rest of the Highlanders were drawn out to see the execution and joined in prayer with great earnestness. The unfortunate men behaved with perfect resolution and propriety. Their bodies were put into three coffins by three of their clansmen and namesakes, and buried in one grave near the place of execution.

The rest of the deserters were drafted to other regiments serving in plague spots and thousands of miles from their native Highlands. At home the men were generally regarded as martyrs to the treachery of the government, which may well have helped Prince Charles, the Young Pretender, two years later.

It is fascinating to wonder what might have happened had The Black Watch been quartered in Aberfeldy and not Flanders in 1745. Anyhow, whatever stain there was on the regiment's record through its first and only mutiny was very soon 'wiped away by blood, battle, and bravery well beyond the call of duty'.

'My Lord, we are damnably cut up.'

The Black Watch, since its formation in the 18th Century, has been committed in so many engagements in so many parts of the world that its history is inextricably interwoven with the history of Britain. The War of American Independence, Napoleon's Egyptian Campaign, Quatre Bras and Waterloo, the Crimea, the Indian Mutiny and the First and Second World Wars – in all these and more, the Black Watch has played a distinguished role.

Black Watch after tidying graveyard. Hong Kong 1997.

(Frank Proctor)

On 15 June 1815, for example, when dawn brought the end of the Duchess of Richmond's Ball in Brussels, the Black Watch were already marching to battle to the tune of *Hielan' Laddie*. And even at such an

early hour there were crowds to see them go and murmur to one another that these charming men with petticoats who, when billeted on the inhabitants, helped to make the soup and rock the cradle for the half-frightened mistress of the family, would be no match for the ferocious warriors of Napoleon's army.

'He's humbugged me, by God!' exclaimed Wellington, when he received reports of Napoleon's actual whereabouts. So, throughout 15 June reserves came hurrying from Brussels. They were a fast moving division made up, mostly, of riflemen and a Highland brigade who were used to trotting along with their 60lb packs. Their speed enabled them to play a crucial role in the overall battle because as they arrived, the hill and farm of Quatre Bras, the main defence, were being overrun.

The 42nd was hurriedly positioned close to the crossroads and at 1600 hrs the French attacked with light infantry. The Black Watch thrust them aside and stormed onwards but Marshal Ney still had his cavalry – Lancers and heavy Cuirassiers. Now, a square is the only way to face cavalry, and to form a square from line the centre ranks stand firm, while the companies on either side fall back to form left and right faces and the two flank companies run in to form the rear. Unfortunately, in this instance, the Lancers' charge, from the rear, arrived before the flank companies could form up and horsemen thundered into the square. In the ensuing carnage, command of the battalion changed hands four times in a few moments of frenzied close-quarter fighting.

The lance is longer than the bayonet and horses are heavier than men but three sides of the square held firm. Turned towards the centre the Highlanders pressed in on the Lancers and – a rare feat – closed its square on the horsemen inside, forcing them to surrender or be killed. One Captain Menzies, six-and-a-half-feet tall, received 17 lance wounds in the mêlée and used to entertain guests at dinner parties afterwards by maintaining that fourteen of them were mortal. He lived to a ripe old age.

That was the light cavalry dealt with but Marshall Ney now spurred on the heavies, the Cuirassiers, telling them 'the fate of France is in your hands'. Two regiments scattered before their charge and it began to look as if they might have some success.

> Our last file had just got back into square when the Cuirassiers dashed full on two of its faces; their heavy horses and steel armour seemed sufficient to bury us had they been pushed forward onto our bayonets.

Then Major Campbell, the new Commanding Officer, gave the order and a lethal volley was fired from close range.

> Riders cased in heavy armour came tumbling from their horses, which reared, plunged and fell on the dismounted riders, steel helmets and cuirasses rang against unsheathed sabres as they fell on the ground.

In their long jackboots and steel breastplates, the horsemen lay upturned, reminding Wellington, who was nearby, of 'so many turned turtles'.

The 42nd's extraordinary resilience, with its incomplete square, under the Lancers' charge and its disciplined fire which broke the Cuirassiers, and the fact that this occurred at the crucial stage of the battle when Marshall Ney was on the point of victory, fully justify Wellington's selection of the regiment as one of only four for special mention in his dispatch from Quatre Bras.

Although not directly involved at Waterloo until late in the battle, the 2nd Battalion of the 73rd – initially the 2nd Battalion of the 42nd – in its turn, played a vital role in the victory. There were three ranks in front of their square, the first two kneeling and the rear standing. Early in the afternoon came the first Cuirassiers' charge. They held their fire until the horsemen were within just ten paces and then the rear rank fired. As the horses wheeled and plunged, the two front ranks each fired in turn, and there was no need for the fourth volley which the rear rank had ready.

When the next charge came, Wellington rode into their square and watched that, too, being repulsed. Then they saw the guns being loaded with grapeshot, the charge rammed home and the touch light applied.

Black Watch sniper.

Hong Kong 1997.

(JSPRS)

The grapeshot scythed great swathes through the ranks, the horsemen galloping up to make use of the gaps. But before they could do so, the 73rd had closed ranks, and the Cuirassiers were again forced to retreat.

Again more grapeshot 'as thick as hail upon us'. Men were falling in dozens at each shot, but with the cavalry so close they could not move or they would be overwhelmed. The Duke of Wellington asked their General how things were going:

'Well, Halkett, how do you get on?'

'My lord, we are damnably cut up; can you not relieve us for a little while?'

'Impossible.'

'Very well, my lord, we'll stand till the last man falls.'

By this time the crux of the battle had been reached. The 73rd's ammunition was all used up, and they could only watch as the Cuirassiers walked their horses up to the Highland bayonet points. But they still could not break through.

At last, Wellington was able to send in his own cavalry. From behind the 73rd, as they pushed determinedly forward, there came the thudding of hooves. With a roar of 'Scotland for Ever!', the Scots Greys came thundering through and, as they passed, the Highlanders plucked at their stirrup leathers to be carried into the fight by those massive horses. Their irresistible surge swept the French infantry off the ridge and into the valley. Later on, the Imperial Guard was thrown at them but even they broke on those immovable squares and, at the end of the day, the 73rd stood within 50 yards of where it had been that morning.

After Waterloo came Paris and the 42nd were again on display. The Parisian ladies admired their manly thighs and, as they keenly eyed them in their kilts, whispered to their friends, 'My dear, if it be windy!' *Plus ça change, plus c'est la même chose?*

Hong Kong Sevens with Pipes and Drums. April 1997.

(Frank Proctor)

Tsar Alexander, if reports are true, went too far. Inspecting six men from the kilted regiments, his curiosity about the famous mystery could not be checked; according to one sergeant who wrote, with justifiable indignation, the Tsar 'pinched my skin, hinting that I wore something

under my kilt and had the curiosity to lift my kilt to my navel that he might not be deceived'.

In December 1815, the 42nd returned to Britain. They marched north through repeated rapturous welcomes until they arrived in Edinburgh 'to the most distinguished reception a regiment had ever had'. A week of celebrations. The seventh evening ended with a speech from Sir Walter Scott and then they marched off unsteadily towards the Castle, 'as if a whirlwind had been blowing amongst us. No lives were lost, though many a bonnet and kilt changed owners'.

CHAPTER 3

TO KEEP SILENT AND ENDURE

We now turn to nearer the beginning of the Hong Kong story, the period when the Western powers first took a serious interest in China and settled the conditions under which they would trade. China seemed a huge untapped market for Western manufactured goods but, over the years, the Imperial Dynasty had stubbornly resisted all attempts to open trading relations. Some foreign merchants had, of course, been permitted to trade in Canton since the 17th Century, a Portuguese ship

The Chinese border from Macao. (Craig)

having cast anchor at Canton in 1615, but the cultural gulf between the two worlds could not have been wider.

Father Matthew Ricci, a Jesuit, who had first learnt Mandarin in Macao (where the Portuguese had been given permission by the Chinese to set up a base in 1557), embarked upon a journey to Peking which, as things turned out, took 20 years to complete. On arrival at the Celestial Throne, he presented a map which displayed five continents. The Chinese believed there was but one continent, and, by 1747, as Scotland lay raw from the consequences of Culloden, the Ming official encyclopaedia dismissed Father Ricci's ideas as 'nothing more than a wild fabulous story'.

At the end of the 18th Century, the Chinese were still certain that their Empire lay at the world's centre and regarded the British as mere 'distant barbarians'. The first official British Mission to China, in 1793, despatched by the government of William Pitt the Younger and seeking improved trading conditions, was unsuccessful.

In the 1830s, the British Superintendent of Trade in Canton, Lord Napier of Merchiston, found the Chinese unwilling to accept his credentials, but quick to see him as a spy – a 'barbarian eye'. To the

Traditional boat, Aberdeen Harbour, Hong Kong. (Craig)

Victorians, in the full flush of the Industrial Revolution, all this seemed grossly inadequate. They determined to get what they wanted and did it by force in the Opium Wars of 1840–42 and later when an Anglo-French force attacked China.

The main concessions they extracted were, in 1841, a settlement in Hong Kong Island and, in 1860, the south Kowloon Peninsula and Stonecutters' Island. The rest of Kowloon and an area north of Kowloon up to the Shenzhen River, the New Territories, was leased from China in 1898 for 99 years, a lease which would run out in 1997. The Chinese authorities were also forced to give up land in certain towns and cities which became small extensions of British territory to be administered in the English way. A further insult to the Chinese was the clause which forced them to allow foreign nationals who committed crimes to be tried by their own national courts. The British were pleased with themselves but for the Chinese – whoever was in power – the overturning of these 'unequal treaties' remained a constant burning ambition.

The decision to move on Tiananmen Square over the weekend of 3–4 June 1989 was probably taken on the previous Friday. Deng Xiaoping

Hakka women, Kam Tin walled village, New Territories. (Craig)

approved it. The 27th and 38th armies of the PLA would carry out the operation. The latter was Beijing's garrison army. Its commander was against the action and was afterwards removed. These troops were strengthened by units from each of China's military districts. Everyone would share responsibility.

As troops began to move about the city two other elements became apparent. An estimated one million young people with no hope of work had congregated in Beijing and there were now considerable numbers of factory and office workers involved. What was alarming about this, to the Old Guard, was that it seemed to be a rising of the proletariat *against* rather than *for* Communism.

The key to discussion of the PLA and China *vis-à-vis* Hong Kong at the time of the handover lies in the events in Tiananmen Square in 1989. And the key to Tiananmen Square is what had occurred in China over previous decades.

The period that followed the overthrow of the Manchu Dynasty in 1912 and led to the establishment of the Chinese People's Republic 37 years later has been a turbulent and traumatic time for the Chinese people. Warlords, Japanese invasion and occupation, civil war between the Communists and Chiang Kaishek's Kuomintang; then, under Communism, self-inflicted famine and the Cultural Revolution, each event leaving that multi-layered country in turmoil.

By the 1900s the Chinese had begun taking back control of their country and, under the leadership of Sun Yat Sen, overthrew the last Emperor of the Manchu Dynasty, Piu Yi, and, on 15 February 1912, a republic was established with Yuan Shi Kai as provisional President. But, alas, the Chinese soon fell out amongst themselves with the South rebelling against the North. Civil war was inevitable.

The First World War hardly involved China though some 200,000 labourers were sent to France to help in transport and construction work, in the hope that a beaten Germany might have to give up its existing concessions and trading privileges. The Treaty of Versailles slammed the door firmly on that idea, giving the German rights in the province of Shantung to Japan. The Chinese response was angry and immediate, making the world aware of their strength of feeling about Japan's aggressive policies.

Meanwhile, in 1920, China's Southern Provinces proclaimed themselves the Independent Republic of Southern China, though this soon became only a loose federation, and Yuan Shi Kai, who had by now ascended the Dragon Throne, died. The era of the warlords had begun.

Between 1924 and 1927, the Kuomintang (Nationalists) joined the Chinese Communist Party in an effort to be more effective revolutionaries. The first priority, of course, was the army and on 9 July 1926 a northern expedition finally got under way, capturing by that autumn, the whole of the upper Yangtse Valley. Chiang Kaishek's forces entered Shanghai in March 1927 with Nanking falling to the Nationalists two days later. So now the Kuomintang and the Communists ruled all China south of the Yangtse. But they were already disenchanted with each other, and the end came in June 1927. The Kuomintang expelled all Soviet advisers from China and a wave of executions in Shanghai caused the Communist leaders to flee. Communists had now become outlaws, to be hunted down and exterminated. Thousands were killed. The Communist forces staged insurrections in various towns and although this revolt was a fiasco, it marked the beginning of the Communist army. The army was small, with limited resources and weapons, but from that time Mao Zedong, its leader, was never without his own troops. He believed that the key to revolutionary success was to rouse the peasants, but first they must be properly armed.

There was disagreement amongst the Nationalists, and it was December 1927 before Chiang Kaishek was able to get on the move again. Within ten months, though, through good luck and Japanese meddling in Shantung, the warlords were beaten, and in October 1928, Chiang was able to establish the National Government of China, with its capital at Nanking, although, in reality, his remit only ran in the lower Yangtse region. Chiang Kaishek's government was recognised by the Western powers, which meant China could make some progress in changing parts of those detested 'unequal treaties' with Britain.

Japan, however, was grimly determined to cling on to what it had, as its policies were firmly expansionist. The question for Tokyo was whether to achieve its aims through diplomacy or war. There was not much room for argument as its government was dominated by the military. In June 1931, three Japanese soldiers in civilian clothes were arrested by the Chinese in a restricted military zone in Manchuria and executed as spies. Some six weeks later the Japanese army struck at Mukden and the 'Manchurian Incident' had begun. Within 12 months, they had overrun almost the whole of Manchuria and set up the puppet state of Manchukuo with Piu Yi, the last Manchu Emperor of China, as ruler. The Japanese in China exhibited the same atrocious cruelty they were to demonstrate a few years later in Hong Kong and elsewhere.

Jinzhou, about which Jung Chang writes in her book *Wild Swans*, was a big city, the capital of one of the nine provinces of Manchukuo, situated about ten miles from the sea. It had a number of textile factories and a couple of oil refineries, was an important railroad junction and had its own airport. It was in a highly strategic location and played a central role in the takeover of Manchuria. It will serve as an example for other towns in other parts of China.

When local children passed a Japanese in the street, they had to bow and make way even if the Japanese was younger than themselves. Japanese children would often stop local children and slap them for no reason at all. The authorities showed newsreels in schools of Japan's progress in the war. Far from being ashamed of their brutality, the Japanese emphasised it as a way of inculcating fear. They showed, for instance, soldiers cutting people in half and prisoners tied to stakes being torn to pieces by dogs. The Japanese teachers watched the children closely to make sure they did not shut their eyes or try to stick a handkerchief in their mouths to stifle their screams. Jung Chang writes that her mother had nightmares for years afterwards.

Torture was frequent. If the Japanese thought a Chinese had money, they would grab him, split his ribs open and pour water into the rib cage to make him tell them where it was hidden. And, often, it was only

39

for fun. On one occasion, a little girl began to cry in fear when she saw some soldiers. This greatly amused them and, dragging her into the street, they danced around, slicing her body with their bayonets. Her screams rent the neighbourhood. Throughout the 20th Century the Chinese have had to learn, time and time again, to keep silent and endure.

The League of Nations protested at such aggression but Tokyo ignored them, and in April 1933 Japanese troops broke through the Great Wall and entered Hopei province. Chiang Kaishek's response was immediate. He agreed to Japanese demands for a demilitarised zone in Hopei and got on with civil war. It was only in 1936, two years after the epic 12-month Long March of over 6,000 miles by the Communists into north-west China, that both sides finally joined forces to fight the invaders. The Long March brought together many people who were to hold leading posts in the future, including Mao Zedong, Zhou Enlai and Deng Xiaoping.

The second Sino-Japanese war began in July 1937, when fighting started near Peking – the so-called 'Peking Incident'. In August there was fighting in Shanghai. Peking fell to the Japanese on 8 August and Shanghai was captured in November. Next, Japanese troops in the south advanced along the Yangtse valley and in December stormed Nanking. The destruction of that city and the excesses committed against its citizens were ghastly and heralded much bushido behaviour to come.

Chiang Kaishek was forced to move his capital up-river to Chungking and it was generally thought that he would now give in to any demands the Japanese might make. But he did not do so, and the war continued. In the autumn of 1938, Hankow and Canton were taken. Once again, Chiang Kaishek refused an offer of peace, though it seemed it would only be a matter of time before the Japanese overran the whole of China.

However, in Europe, the beginning of the Second World War actually marked the end of Japan's successes in China, though they were not to know that until the bombs of Hiroshima and Nagasaki. It also signalled the end of Chiang Kaishek though no one would have bet on that at the time.

Japan's war plans to break the Western powers' hold on Asia led to a pre-emptive attack on the US Pacific Fleet at Pearl Harbour on 7 December 1941. On 8 December 1941 they bombed Hong Kong and up to 15,000 ground troops arrived from the north to dislodge the British and the Canadians from Kowloon and the New Territories. On 18/19 December, as the British refused to surrender, the Japanese invaded Hong Kong Island. On Christmas Day, the British and the Canadians surrendered. Survivors of the multi-national garrison were brutally treated or killed, nursing sisters being raped and murdered.

Three quarters of the Chinese population were forcibly repatriated. Hong Kong was not liberated until 30 August 1945.

CHAPTER 4

USELESSLY SACRIFICED?

I n 1937, the regiment became The Black Watch (Royal Highland Regiment) reverting, in the brackets, to the old title given to it after Fontenoy by King George II. This remains its full formal name.

Across the Channel, Germany was building U boats, tanks and aeroplanes. And Britain? When the 1st Battalion went on manoeuvres in August 1938, it had 22 Bren guns instead of 50. Its anti-tank rifles were represented by lengths of gas piping stuck into pieces of wood. Blue flags were the symbols for the Bren-gun carriers it did not have. It

Black Watch Guard,
Prince of Wales
Barracks. 1997.

(Frank Proctor)

had neither mortars nor anti-tank guns; nor even flags to represent them. And it could muster less than 300 all ranks. These manoeuvres were watched by an interested group of military attachés from Italy, Egypt and Germany amongst others.

Thus, when war eventually came – nearly coinciding with the regiment's 200th anniversary – strange new jobs and new military thinking had to be learned in a hurry. And the kilt had to be handed in to Ordinance in return for regular battle-dress. As Bernard Fergusson writes in his book *The Black Watch and the King's Enemies*, 'arguments for and against the kilt are legion, but from the point of view of morale, a man in a kilt is a man and a half, and the men took the news very ill'. The afternoon that the order was issued, their Majesties the King and Queen drove over from Windsor to see the battalion. The King took the salute and then said to the Queen: 'This is your Regiment: you inspect it.'

Five of Her Majesty The Queen Mother's family, the Bowes-Lyons, have served in the Black Watch and a cousin, as well as her brother, was killed in the First World War. It is impossible to describe the affection the regiment has for its Colonel-in-Chief but it has flourished, mutually, for over 60 years.

Both their Majesties talked at length and with sympathy about the loss of the kilt. It was given out that one of the main reasons for withdrawing it was to prevent the regiment from being identified. 'But damn it!' said Big Mac, alias CSM MacGregor, 'we *want* to be identified!' It would in fact have been very unpleasant to be kilted in France that winter but, and not for the first or last time, the manner of its abandonment was insensitive and stupid.

In January 1940, the 51st Highland Division landed in France, and the 4th and 6th Battalions (Territorial) with it. Its commander, General Victor Fortune, was a renowned Black Watch character. He was the only officer of the regiment who, coming to France with the 1st Battalion in 1914, went straight through to the end of the war without a scratch.

In February it was decided that each brigade of the Highland Division should have one regular battalion in it, and the 1st Battalion was to be one of them. Unfortunately, the battalion it was to displace was the 6th

Black Watch. So, on 4 March, the two battalions changed over. The 6th now took the 1st Battalion's place in the 4th Division with which it was to fight in France, Tunisia and Italy, finishing the war in Greece. The 1st Battalion's destiny was to be very different.

From the mouth of the Somme to the little port of Saint-Valéry is roughly 60 miles. The coastline is mostly cliffs, with tiny fishing harbours and, here and there, stretches of beach rather like the east coast of Scotland. Some 25 miles inland is the main Abbeville road to Le Havre and it was inside this corridor, that over the next 12 days, the Division began its impossible fight. There are some rivers in this 'corridor' – the Bresle, the Bethune and the Varenne – which look, on the map, as though they might provide obstacles for an advancing enemy but it is an illusion and the only river that could cause problems was the Somme and the Germans already had a bridgehead at Abbeville. Thus, everything depended on whether this bridgehead could be reduced or destroyed.

The divisional reconnaissance regiment was the Lothians and Border Horse equipped with light tanks. Bernard Fergusson records in *The Black Watch and the King's Enemies*, the scathing words of a passing Jock: 'Ca' thae things tanks? They're knockin' them oot three a penny up the road yonder'.

The failure of a combined British/French attack enabled the Germans to build up their strength in the bridgehead and to withstand another assault on 4 June without much trouble. Next day they themselves attacked and the long, painful withdrawal to Saint-Valéry began.

Communications, an essential ingredient for success, were a nightmare. There was to be no more rest until the end, except for the odd hour snatched from time to time or the exhausted sleep into which men fell in the middle of their work, or even on the march. Changes of orders came too frequently, always arriving at the last moment and requiring alterations of rendezvous for companies which messages could not reach because they were already on their way There were no radios, no field telephones. Dispatch riders were the only means of keeping contact and they could easily get lost, particularly in the dark, and sometimes they simply disappeared without trace. Soon they had to be replaced by officers, who were in increasingly short supply. There were only five maps for the whole battalion and these, anyway, showed only the main roads. The miracle is not that there was such confusion but that the battalion retained any coherence at all.

General Fortune had already asked for permission to embark his force at Dieppe, but the War Office, loyal to the British alliance with the French, had ruled that the Highland Division must continue to support them. They were to move to a line some two miles from Saint-Valéry and hold themselves in readiness. More confusion followed, with delays adding greatly to the difficulties. Equipment had to be abandoned and destroyed, and with each delay came amended orders. However, in spite of this, the battalion reached Saint-Pierre-le-Vique, six miles from Saint-Valéry, more or less complete.

Eventually, on 12 June, the Division was squeezed back into Saint-Valéry. Tanks and heavy mortars pounded them from three sides. They had no food, no water and only such ammunition as they could find lying abandoned. Groups of French soldiers wandering across their front with white flags did not help and the Navy was powerless to take off what remained of the Division. There was nothing left to fight for and early in the morning, acting on orders from London, General Fortune surrendered to the German General whose troops surrounded him – Erwin Rommel.

By leaving the 51st Highland Division in France after Dunkirk to fight a battle that could not be won, the British government showed it was ready to risk losing it for political ends. It was determined to stick by the policy of appearing to support the French through thick and thin, even though most of the signals Churchill was getting from France spelt out that defeat was inevitable and that there would soon be an armistice. It may even be that the Division was deliberately sacrificed as a symbol of Allied unity which would silence French complaints that Britain had abandoned them.

The late Duke of Argyll, Captain Ian Campbell in 1940 and General Fortune's Intelligence Officer, speaking many years later, had this to say:

It has always been abundantly clear to me that no Division has ever been more uselessly sacrificed. It could have been got away a good week

before, but the powers-that-be – and owing, I think, to very faulty information – had come to the conclusion that there was a capacity for resistance in France which was not actually there.

'And there my comrades sleep ...'

In September 1941, the 2nd Battalion The Black Watch was moved to Tobruk from Syria to relieve the 9th Australian Division. They did not like what they found. Water was scarce, and brackish; it was drinkable only in tea 'and, possibly in

Rest on launch between
rehearsals.

(Craig)

Simon Weston visits
the Battalion during
training. 1997.

(Frank Proctor)

whisky, if you could get the whisky'. Washing was done in sea water when it could be obtained, which was seldom. Once a fortnight, the NAAFI could supply one razor-blade per section of troops and a twist of boiled sweets for every two or three men, with very occasional cigarettes. The diet was bully beef, tinned fish and biscuits.

On 7 November the battalion was withdrawn, but not for a rest period. It was an open secret that a sortie was planned in which the battalion was to have a leading role, and on 10 November the plan was first explained to company commanders in general terms. Initially it seemed complicated, as the terrain was just desert with nothing but bits of wire to identify features, but the information that a generous allotment of infantry tanks was going to be in support made matters seem rosier.

On 13 November a practice attack was carried out at the precise time at which the real attack was intended, and over similar ground. The joining up was practised in the dark, as it would have to be on the actual day, and 'at zero hour the tanks duly rumbled through, advanced on to the "objective" and everybody felt much better'. The battalion's ultimate objective was an area called 'Tiger' with another called 'Jill' as an intermediate.

General Scobie, who commanded the garrison and the Division as well, made a speech to all the officers, saying that they were being called upon to do a most difficult and hazardous job, but that if anybody could do it, the Black Watch could. He also assured them that the sortie would only be ordered if the German armoured divisions ahead of them had been thoroughly pounded and smashed. Bernard Fergusson writes:

> The prevailing mood was therefore mixed. The importance of the operation, and its hazards, were fully recognised. There was also a lively hope that this might be the heave which was finally going to get the Germans on the run, and that once on the run, they might struggle in vain to regain a foothold until they were engulfed by the Atlantic.

On 20 November at 5.15pm, the long-awaited signal was received and the battalion moved off. Behind them, the usual night air-raid was going on over the harbour and, out in front, no-man's-land was a mass of flares. The Intelligence Officer met each company at a rendezvous and directed it onto a line of white tapes which led to a point near the joining up position. Blankets arrived and everybody tried to get some sleep; but because of the bitterly cold night and the thought of what dawn might bring, not many men slept. At 4.30am there was a whispered reveille, and an issue of tea and rum. Then, along more tapes, the battalion shuffled in the dark, through gaps in the minefield, over the anti-tank ditch and out into the bleakness of no-man's-land.

Zero hour had been fixed for 0630 hrs. The battalion was right up to time but for some reason the tanks were late. The guns were to fire on 'Jill' from zero until zero plus eight minutes. This made it all the more important that the leading troops should not wait for them but start off on time. It would be bad enough attacking without tanks, and it was now more important than ever that they should reap the full benefit of the Royal Horse Artillery (RHA) guns.

So, B Company started off, feeling 'disconsolate and unhappy without the promised tanks, but moving at a brisk pace'. The tanks then arrived four minutes late and unfortunately compounded the error by crossing the anti-tank ditch by the wrong bridge, setting off into no-man's-land on a course too far eastward. B Company advanced for several hundred yards without problems and then 'it was as if all heaven and earth had opened up,' as Fergusson recalls in his account. There were no tanks between them and the enemy objective.

There was nothing for it but to go in with the bayonet. There was no help to be looked for from the tanks now bearing down on the position from the wrong direction. They had got themselves on to a minefield and three or four had already gone up.

B Company went in with a series of rushes. It felt like 'pressing against a solid wall of lead' and it seemed almost impossible that anybody should survive. When, after 40 minutes, 'Jill' had been overrun, there was nothing left of the company to carry on to the main objective. Of the five officers, three had been killed and two wounded, one mortally. Of the 13 NCOs, seven were dead or wounded.

There were still no tanks to lead the assault on to 'Tiger'. B Company's rapid advance had left several pockets of resistance behind it, and the hail of bullets from 'Jill' had cut many gaps in the other advancing companies.

Large numbers of German prisoners were surrendering but scant attention was paid to them. 'Tiger' was the objective. The CSM of B Company, with the ten men who were all that he could muster, pushed on in D Company's wake as they passed through.

The other companies came on behind, and from their midst rose the sound of the pipes. Ever since the 2nd Battalion had arrived in Tobruk, the pipes had been forbidden, but nothing could muffle them now; they were playing the battalion in. A major of the Royal Horse Artillery who saw the whole action wrote:

> I class this attack of the Black Watch as one of the most outstanding examples of gallantry combined with high-class training that I have seen. Not one of us who was there will ever forget such supreme gallantry.

Black Watch soldier in training, 'proud and privileged'. 1997.

(Frank Proctor)

But the horror was not yet over; indeed, the worst was still to come. For, as the companies pressed on beyond 'Jill' the gunfire became devastating. A German machine-gun battalion was sited in and around 'Tiger'. There were shells, mortars and small arms fire.

The signal for stretcher-bearers was a rifle stuck into the ground by its bayonet, and soon there was a forest of them. There were still no tanks. The enemy fire was cutting not gaps but swathes in the battalion's ranks. The few surviving officers, out of touch with one another but realising the extent of the devastation, came individually to the same conclusion – that they must call a halt until there was some tank support. Machine-guns on fixed lines were sending their bullets whipcracking through the air and the number of men still on their feet was derisory.

It was the commanding officer, Colonel Rusk, who saved the situation. He realised that everything hinged on getting the tanks back on to their objective. Having had two vehicles shot from under him, he went off after the tanks in a third, attracted their attention and diverted them on to 'Tiger'. Standing up in one of them like a policeman, he returned to the companies and ordered them on. Behind the tanks the advance resumed and 'Tiger' was occupied.

In one single bloody hour, the 2nd Battalion had been reduced to a quarter of its strength; out of 32 officers and 600 men, eight officers and 160 men were all that was left. Two of the companies had no officers at all, whilst one had fewer than ten men and was being commanded by its CSM.

> Remote from pilgrimage, a dusty hollow
> > Lies in the Libyan plain:
> And there my comrades sleep, who will not follow
> > The pipes and drums again:
> Who followed closely in that desperate sally
> > The pipes that went before;
> Who, heedless now of Muster or Reveille,
> > Sleep sound for ever more ...

... Far off in Scotland at the hour of battle,
    As these her sons fell dead,
Above the herds of frosty-breathing cattle
    The winter sun rose red:
In every cothouse and in every city
    In those remembered shires,
The kettle sang its early morning ditty
    On newly kindled fires ...

... To those dear houses with their chimneys reeking
    In Angus or in Fife,
No spirit came, its words of omen speaking,
    To mother or to wife;
Yet in the nameless desert to the southward
    Before the sun was high,
The husbands whom they loved, the sons they mothered
    Stood up and went to die.

                    Bernard Fergusson, 1941
(Written after a visit to the area a few days after the Tobruk breakout.)

Captain David Rose, later to command the 1st Battalion in Korea, was sent from Cairo to Tobruk with reinforcements and was immediately made Adjutant. On the day of his arrival Colonel Rusk had to visit the forward companies and David Rose went with him. As they walked the CO asked Rose whether he was used to being under fire. Rose replied that he had been under very light artillery fire in Somaliland for one day. 'Well, walk behind me and do as I do.' They had not gone very far when there was the loud crack of an 88mm German AA gun. Captain Rose described the occasion:

Rusky dived for a hole in the ground. It was all so sudden that I was left standing, fortunately, for my poor Colonel had chosen an Italian shit trench for cover. I pulled him out and did my best to scrape off the horrors to very little effect, so we had to go on to Major TE's dug-

Highland Band favourites. Rehearsals, June 1997. (JSPRS)

out in a sorry state ... I asked him to find some water and a stiff brush. It was no use; it just spread the muck around and made it worse. Rusky took it all very philosophically and decided to return to his own HQ in woollen vest and long johns, just as though nothing had happened.

The Colonel would not talk about the battle and Captain Rose knew he was grieving.

In my view the battle had been a balls up and, except for George Rusk's personal bravery, might have been a complete disaster. The planning was faulty. Where had the Brigade Major been trained? Did he know about marches, guides and tapes for night attacks? What about the tank Squadron Commander? Had he ever been taught how to use a compass? His troop was not only very late on the start line but went out on the wrong bearing. He was a rather 'Tally-ho, a-hunting we shall go' sort of fellow. I thought there should be some form of enquiry so that it didn't happen again. But no ..., the book was to be closed; no post-mortem.

' ... there came the sound of the pipes.'

Meanwhile, a new Highland Division had been formed. The calamity of Saint-Valéry had been a national blow. Eric Linklater, himself a former Black Watch soldier, wrote that 'to Scotland the news came like another Flodden. Scotland is a small country; and in its northern half there was hardly a household that had not at least a cousin in one of the Highland Regiments'.

The process of rebuilding the Division began under Major General Neil Ritchie, of the Black Watch Regiment, but it was under Major General Douglas Wimberley of the Camerons that the division (which included the 1st, 5th and 7th Battalions of the Black Watch) was finally – two years to the month after Saint-Valéry – trained and ready for revenge. The arrival of the Highland Division in Egypt coincided, more or less, with the arrival of Generals Alexander and Montgomery, and as that partnership swept the war forward, the Highland Division went with it, always near the van of the onward movement, and sharing in the 8th Army's newly-acquired reputation.

The Battle of Alamein was imminent. Commanding Officers were warned some days before the actual battle that they were to take part in the coming assault but were not allowed to tell the men until 21 October. Then the task allotted to each company was explained to them with the help of sand models.

On the night of 22 October, all the troops involved moved into prepared assembly areas, consisting of quantities of slit trenches, each to shelter two men and camouflage them from the air. When dawn came up on 23 October the enemy had no indication that the desert in front of the German positions was any more populated than it had been the evening before. But every trench now held two men, each with a full supply of ammunition, hard rations and water. All day they lay there, waiting for nightfall and the advance. They were forbidden to move from the trenches so the strain of waiting can be imagined. When darkness fell, the men were able to get up, stretch their legs and eat a hot meal brought up from the rear.

The 5th Battalion was on the extreme right of the Division, shoulder to shoulder with the Australians; the 7th was on the extreme left, beside the New Zealanders. Each battalion had to pass through the forward areas and the gaps in the British minefield to reach the Start Line. There they waited, in darkness and in silence. According to Bernard Fergusson:

> It was a perfectly ordinary night. There was no noise, no sign of apprehension on the part of the enemy. There was nothing to show that in that moment the war was crossing its watershed. And then, at 2140 hrs, the sky was ripped for 50 miles to south and north with shell fire ... At first the gun-flashes flickered silently in the sky like Northern Lights. Then came the noise; and in a few moments the huge moon, privy to the plot, was blotted out by the smoke and dust of explosions. In the occasional second between the bursting and whistling of shells there came the sound of the pipes, from end to end of the advancing line of the Highland Division.

Navigating officers trod warily ahead with compasses, leading the way through the complex maze of minefields and booby-traps. One company encountered wire and it so happened that the company barber had been entrusted with the wire-cutters. 'Get a bluidy move on, Jock,' shouted a voice in the night. 'You're no cuttin' hair noo.'

And so they advanced to punch a corridor deep through the enemy positions and minefields to let the tanks pass out into the open desert. Piper McIntyre was hit three times but played on as he lay dying on the ground. When he was found next morning the bag was still under his arm, the blow-stick still between his lips, his stiff fingers still on the chanter. He was 19 years old.

The 7th Battalion had taken no part in this initial advance. Its role was to pass through the objectives of the other battalions of the Highland Division and to thrust at the feature known in the division as 'The Ben'. This they did, but only after the plan had been amended because of the heavy shelling and mortaring, which increased as they advanced. The second minefield too, was a mass of booby-traps, worse than the one which the 1st Battalion had passed through.

Such was the first phase of the Highland Division's share in the Battle of Alamein. Thereafter, everybody moved to the second phase which

General Montgomery had termed 'the dog-fight'. Now the Highland Division pounded in pursuit of Rommel's *Afrika Corps*. They learned to work with tanks, to ride on tanks, to use wrecked tanks as pill-boxes. Tripoli was captured in January 1943. And, in Tunisia, all three battalions fought at Medenine, which broke the Mareth line, near the border between Tunisia and Tripolitania, which had been built by the French. After this battle nothing could stop the Eighth Army from joining up with the 1st Army from the west, which included the 6th Battalion Black Watch.

At Wadi Akarit three Black Watch battalions fought side by side in a short, bloody, all-day battle. General Wimberley has said it was the finest fought by the Division in North Africa or Sicily. The weight of the day fell on the individual soldiers in their sections as tanks and wireless sets were knocked out early on. The 7th Battalion lost 11 officers and 180 men but, on the credit side, captured 1,000 prisoners, 56 big guns and a massive collection of small-arms.

After the end of the African campaign, the Highland Division began rehearsing for new style Combined Operations – an amphibious invasion – in a vast fleet of 'Ducks' (DUKW) brought over from America. On 10 July they landed in Sicily. It was a black night and blowing a gale. The ships were packed, and most men were horribly sea-sick. Someone actually died from sea-sickness before he could be landed. Nevertheless, the beaching itself went well. The Black Watch had tough battles at Vizzini and Gerbini but by the middle of August the Germans had been swept out of Sicily. The Highland Division then crossed over to Italy albeit briefly, and then headed for home to prepare for the final part of their journey and the biggest amphibious invasion of all.

In April, the Division moved to East Anglia and tight security set in. Firstly leave was stopped, then mail, and at the end of May and the beginning of June, the Division moved off to a concentration area on the northern shores of the Thames estuary. Then, on 6 June, came the Normandy landings and the 1st, 5th and 7th Battalions Black Watch were soon ashore. For a month of heavy scrapping, the three battalions held positions around the River Orne. Then they all took part in the break-out from Caen, and the drive to Falaise, powering southwards in armoured personnel carriers by the light of searchlights reflected off the clouds. Tanks moving on the flank of the advance fired tracers to show the general direction.

And then, 51 months after that bitter disaster, the 51st Highland Division came back to Saint-Valéry. They were very different. They had learned to co-operate in close teamwork with aircraft, artillery and armour and become polished in the complicated patterns of modern war. But, as the massed pipes and drums beat retreat outside the Château at Cailleville, they were as one with their comrades of 1940. Major General Thomas Rennie – one of the original officers who had returned to the Division when it was training in Scotland, who had been with it when it fought in Africa and Sicily and commanded it while it took its revenge in Normandy – had this to say:

> That Highland Division was Scotland's pride; and its loss, and with it the magnificent men drawn from practically every town, village and croft in Scotland, was a great blow … It has been our task to avenge the fate of our less fortunate comrades and that we have nearly accomplished … We have lived up to the traditions of the 51st and of Scotland.

On the night of 22 March 1945, the 7th Battalion The Black Watch had the satisfaction of knowing that their signal reporting that they were safely over the Rhine was the first to be received. Later that same day, as the morning mist was lifting, Major General Rennie was killed.

Bernard Fergusson:

> His courage was far beyond the ordinary, but there was nothing flamboyant about him. From being the ideal adjutant, he became in turn the ideal staff officer, commanding officer, brigade commander and finally division commander. Like Victor Fortune he became a legend in his lifetime; and there was no Jock in the division who did not know his duffle-coated figure. He never wore a red hat to the day of his death. A Red Hackle was good enough for him.

*Black Watch practice for
Dragon Boat Race.
1997. (JSPRS)*

*1800 hrs ceremony at
the Cenotaph, Hong
Kong. 1997.*
(Frank Proctor)

CHAPTER 5

A ROUND PEG

T he Reverend Peter Ellis is Senior Chaplain at the Hong Kong
Mariners' Club in Middle Road, Kowloon, and, to quote one of his
pamphlets, the sea is his parish. He has been an Anglican priest for over
25 years, working also in Britain and Singapore, and he has been in Hong
Kong, the third largest port and the largest container port in the world, for
five years with eight more to go. His wife, too, is part of the parish, in that
she teaches at a school in Stanley, Hong Kong Island, which trains boys
for a life at sea. His warm Welsh voice came over the telephone:

> 'Good morning ... there's had to be a bit of a change ... I've got some
> other people as well ... But if you'd like to go on the water just turn
> up. Don't bother to ring again ... Sorry to mess you about.'

Now, at this stage of our stay in Hong Kong, with the humidity almost
at record levels and the green, sparkling South China Sea beckoning
every day, this was like asking a Hong Konger in Central if he wanted
to make some money; not to mention the fact that I'd spent my youth
pottering in small boats around a West Argyll sea-loch and had been
desperate to be on the water in any shape or form, if our busy schedule
would only allow it. Now we could spend a whole morning afloat as
'work'.

And so it was we found ourselves creaming across Victoria Harbour

The Rev. Peter Ellis,
Senior Chaplain with
the Missions to Seamen,
Hong Kong. (Craig)

aboard *The Flying Angel*, the Mission to Seamen's launch, in the company of as inspiring a skipper as one might come across on many a long voyage.

We were to learn that changing plans was an everyday occurrence for the Rev. Ellis and that in this case, after we had arranged to accompany him ship visiting, three events had intervened.

A woman from Newfoundland, on a short stopover on her way to Japan had been knocked down by a bus and, though not in danger, had been very unlucky in the extent of her injuries. So her brother had flown post-haste to Hong Kong and Peter Ellis was looking after him, as he seemed in shock. And not without reason. Apparently he had received a telephone call from Hong Kong in the small hours, asking him if he could 'come over and see his sister's body'. Jolted into complete wakefulness he asked the caller to repeat the message and got the same awful request. Thinking to some purpose, in the midst of his horror, he suddenly asked, on a wild chance, if 'the body' could speak to him on the telephone. 'Certainly,' came the reply, 'I'll just connect you up!'

So he was in Hong Kong making arrangements for his sister – whose hospital stay was turning out to be longer than expected – and trying to deal with insurance matters and Peter Ellis was helping with advice and comfort.

The second event was the arrival in Hong Kong of a Dutch woman and her daughter who, on their way to Japan via a container vessel, had decided to prolong their stay and somehow – we weren't told and we didn't ask – had come within the Mariner's Club orbit and had been invited for a *Flying Angel* cruise.

Thirdly, a Turkish seaman had injured an arm, been taken ashore for hospital treatment and now had to get back aboard his ship as it was due to sail that very day.

Meeting at the Mariners' Club, we walked to the small pier opposite the Cultural Centre and boarded the launch, heading off past Stonecutters' Island towards Tsuen Wan and, as we sliced through the water, we learned something about the Missions to Seamen, modern merchant shipping and – Hong Kong's *raison d'être* since 1841 – the port. The Missions to Seamen is an Anglican charity which has been helping the seafarers of the world since 1856, inspired by the work of the Rev. John Ashley who, 20 years earlier, had pioneered a ministry to seafarers in the Bristol Channel. The story goes that, while out walking with his little son, the child had pointed to a sailing ship and asked how the sailors managed to get to church. This question set him thinking and he later began a voluntary ministry, which, when he had to retire due to ill health, was taken up by others who founded the Missions to Seamen. They adopted a flying angel as their symbol and that symbol is known today to sailors throughout the world. There has been a Mission in Hong Kong since 1885, caring for seamen away from home, regardless of race, colour or creed, as individuals, as children of God.

Today, Peter Ellis said, a large crew does not sail a 'romantic' ship. The 36,000 ships calling at Hong Kong annually are often huge container boxes which move at the press of a button. Where there were, maybe, 40 men on a ship before, now there may be only 14. Technology has gone afloat. Some shipping lines have a good leave system, others do not. And social pressure increases under parallel commercial pressures. The owner wants his cargoes moved from port to port as quickly as possible, which means that container ships may now only be in port for perhaps 24 hours, giving no time at all for socialising, sorting out domestic worries or work grievances. Enter the Mission Chaplain.

This Mission Chaplain then broke off to point out various features of the new Lantau Bridge, which connects the mainland to the new Chek Lap Kok airport on Lantau Island. It is particularly spectacular looking up from water level, but the inhabitants of Discovery Bay, Lantau Island, would soon be fed up, he said, as flats were being built on the opposite shore to house people working on the new MTR line that is being built to the airport. The blocks would still have gaps between them to let evil spirits through – a deadly serious requirement even in cosmopolitan Hong Kong.

With so much ship visiting, does he enjoy the sea in all its different moods? No, he thrives on his work but has no real affinity for the sea. 'The ships don't interest me so much either,' he admits. 'It's the people. There's something special about the seafarer and the seafaring community.' So, it comes as no surprise that he felt the best Hong Kong Handover Ceremony had been put on by the Royal Navy. The closing down of HMS *Tamar* was the most moving of all the farewell ceremonies. The closing of the gates for the very last time and the lowering of the

FSA Sir Percivale with one patrol boat from the Hong Kong Squadron at HMS Tamar, Stonecutters' Island. 1997. (Frank Proctor)

61

flags were beautifully carried out. The first HMS *Tamar* to come to Hong Kong was the fourth ship of that name. She arrived in 1907 as the Royal Navy depot ship and was scuttled in 1941 to prevent her capture by the Japanese. The fifth HMS *Tamar* was the naval shore base.

Seafarers are a section of the community most of us seldom think about. Although ships bring us many vital everyday products – from petrol to food – few people pause to think about who and what is involved in bringing them across the oceans. We just pile up the supermarket trolley and move on. But there are problems. Rust-bucket ships, crooked owners, stranded crews, and 'flags of convenience', those paper refuges for ship owners seeking protection from burdensome regulations like income tax, wage scales, safety. If crews come from Third World countries, desperate for work, owners will pay what they think they can get away with and, consequently, Chaplains end up spending a lot of time trying to help crew members get fair treatment and reasonable conditions.

Peter Ellis told us that the Mission had done 'at least one far-sighted thing' in setting up a second, smaller club, at 2, Container Port Road, Kwai Chung, when the container port was small. Now that it has grown so large, it is wonderful to have the second facility right on the doorstep for visiting seamen. 'They don't know who they work for,' he says. 'Being away longer, not knowing that there is any continuity of work, where they'll be next year or whether somebody will replace them, are great concerns.'

'No other group of individuals has a better insight on the human side of shipping than Port Chaplains,' says Doug Stevenson, director of the Seamen's Church Institute's (New York and New Jersey) Centre for Seafarers' Rights. Because Port Chaplains are trusted and such an institution in the maritime world, seafarers disclose things to them they won't tell anyone else. I don't think there is anywhere the Church is more a necessary part of an industry than it is in the maritime industry, every bit as necessary and legitimate as ship owners' agents and cargo shippers.'

By this time we were approaching the Iranian cargo ship of which the young Turk was a crew member and gave them a siren blast to announce our arrival. But nothing, absolutely nothing, stirred and one got the feeling of a latter day *Mary Celeste*. 'Take the launch to the other side,' directed the chaplain and we churned round the freighter's bows to come alongside a rather rusty support ship with a single Chinese face peering out of a window. After a few inconclusive exchanges, it was decided that the young seaman would board the support vessel first and then clamber aboard the freighter. He seemed confident about this, so we shook hands all round and, with a final blast of the siren, set off back towards Hong Kong Island via Kap Shui Mun channel and under the shorter section of the Lantau Bridge.

Next we arrived at Aberdeen Harbour, teeming with boats from the highly luxurious to the strictly functional. The launch tied up at 'Jumbo's', the huge floating restaurant and, as we stepped ashore, realising just how hot it was without the sea breezes and the ship's awning, Peter Ellis asked if we would fancy a lager. A lager! We all immediately became John Mills in the famous 1950s film *Ice Cold in Alex*.

We all piled ashore in high expectation but by the time we were climbing the last flight of stairs towards the bar, the Chaplain appeared going in the opposite direction and murmuring that in order to make it in time for the brother of the injured lady from Newfoundland to keep his legal appointment, we must start for home straightaway. I followed the others slowly, hoping my face didn't reflect my feelings.

So it was briskly back, past a wonderful variety of craft, to disembark at the Cultural Centre steps and go our separate ways: 'Mr Newfoundland' to his lawyer, the chaplain and the Dutch women to Dim Sum, which we had to miss as we had a visit to the Legislative Council arranged. So we ended up hungry as well as thirsty.

Peter Ellis told us there was a lot of Christian activity in Hong Kong through various societies, charities and so on. He mentioned the St Stephen's Society, Jackie Pullinger with her work amongst drug addicts which she has written about so vividly in her book *Chasing the Dragon* and 'Outreach' which helps children in distress. The Jockey Club, which has the monopoly on all gambling in the territory, is legally obliged to use its profits for charitable purposes and they have built or financed clinics, schools and other institutions all over Hong Kong. In the Chapel he showed us a plaque to the memory of Chinese sailors killed during the Falklands War aboard the Fleet Supply Auxiliary *Sir Galahad*. There had recently been a fine memorial service – and a splendid party – with survivors and others attending, including the Captain who, by coincidence, was now Captain of the *Sir Percivale*, the FSA which had helped to evacuate the garrison at the end of June.

Another story: the children from the Stanley school, at which Mrs Ellis teaches, were invited to a party on board the *Sir Percivale* and set a task – which had been given to other national groups – to reassemble some gun parts. The Chinese children stunned the crew by the speed with which they solved the problem, far faster than any other nationality. So they tried them again with another problem. Same result.

'Yes ... I love Hong Kong. I love Asia': the Rev. Peter Ellis in answer to our final question. He obviously does. It was a delight to meet such an effective round peg in such an essential round hole.

CHAPTER 6

LIBERATE THE LITTLE DEVILS

When the defeated Japanese army left Jinzhou, Manchuria, in 1945, its place was taken by the Soviets, the Chinese Communists and the Kuomintang in quick succession. The latter much impressed the citizens. As Jung Chang says, 'This army had clean uniforms and gleaming new American weapons. These soldiers really looked like an army that had beaten the Japanese, unlike the scruffy Communists.' There was a celebratory feeling in the town, and people flocked to invite troops to stay in their homes. It was felt that these soldiers would maintain law and order and ensure peace at last.

But soon the Kuomintang's position began to deteriorate because of military mistakes and corruption. Inflation rose to just over 100,000 per cent by the end of 1947 – and it was to reach 2,870,000 per cent by the end of 1948. For the civilian population the situation was desperate, as more and more food went to the army, only to be sold back on the black market.

Eventually, the Communists again encircled Jinzhou and got ready to attack. It was a vicious battle. The final attack lasted some 31 hours and, some say, was in many ways the turning point of the whole civil war. The Kuomintang lost 20,000 killed with over 80,000 captured.

And so the Communists were back in Jinzhou again. It was their policy not to kill people who surrendered and to treat prisoners reasonably well. This they hoped would win over the ordinary soldiers, most of whom were poor peasants. It proved very successful, and more and more Kuomintang soldiers let themselves be captured.

The Communists also set about getting the city functioning again, which they did with remarkable speed, bringing food prices under control and issuing relief grain, salt and coal to the poor. This greatly impressed the citizens. Furthermore, their troops were disciplined: 'We won't harm you. We are *your* army, the *people's* army.' There was no looting or raping, and there were constant examples of excellent behaviour. By 1945, the Chinese Communist army numbered an estimated 900,000 troops.

In Beijing, on 1 October 1949, Mao Zedong announced the People's Republic of China, and Chiang Kaishek fled to the island of Formosa (Taiwan). There was progress, however uneven, over the next decade, but it was not fast enough for Mao. The intractable problem of feeding China's ever-increasing population haunted him and, in the late 1950s, believing in the power of mass movements, he decided to place the huge rural population under a giant commune system – the 'Great Leap Forward'. He believed it would solve China's main problem at a stroke. He was self-confident, stubborn and arrogant and entirely sure of his

Fruit stall, Lamma Island. (Craig)

own judgement. The peasants were marshalled into egalitarian units and no longer permitted to have any private property. They had to work together, in a military fashion, dress in blue tunics, men and women both, and eat communally. As someone said 'they owned their chopsticks and not much else'. They never saw any cash.

It is difficult to know what food there was in the late 1950s, but by 1959 the government was sending grain to shortfall areas and local party officials were afraid to report the truth. They might lose their jobs or their lives. So they always sent in higher production figures so that their areas were sent correspondingly inadequate amounts of relief.

By the winter of 1960 starvation was rife and the government began shipping grain to the worst-hit areas by truck. It was often dumped on the roadside for anyone to come and get – if they had the strength. Estimates of deaths resulting from the 'Great Leap Forward' vary from 30 – 46 million. Mao never admitted the policy had been a mistake and never apologised. This would be against Marxist principles.

For one hundred years, Deng Xiaoping said later, the people of China had been at war in one way or another. They had led a life of heavy labour and bitter hardship. Now, instead of finding help and improvements through Communism, they had been plunged into a new and lower circle of hell.

Mao had made a huge misjudgement but no one publicly challenged the commune plans or the Great Leap Forward because, by 1958, it was difficult to tell him anything he did not want to hear. Mao had become infallible. Even Deng Xiaoping, who was later to reap such swift success by reversing the process, stayed silent. It was safer.

But this situation unfortunately only reinforced the attitudes that gave Mao licence for his next epoch-making episode, the 'Great Proletarian Cultural Revolution'. In 1962, Mao turned over economic planning to Liu Shaogi and Deng Xiaoping, giving them a free rein for five years. This seems surprising, but he knew that both Liu and Deng guessed the parlous state the country was in. China was bankrupt.

Deng and Liu bought six million tons of grain on the world market because they had to have quick results. Millions could not go on starving.

The South China Sea.

(Craig)

Deng felt that if he could get things moving, start factories up again and feed the people, it did not matter if he veered away from pure Communism. 'Communism is not poverty ... It does not matter whether the cat is black or white. So long as it catches the mouse it is a good cat.'

This was whipping the carpet from under Mao's feet with a vengeance. He bided his time, plotting his comeback. Had he died in 1956 he would have been hailed as one of China's greatest leaders. Some say he saw power shifting away from him and took an enormous risk to win it back; but others say his actions reflected his frustration with Russia and the deep disagreements between the two countries. He was also frustrated with China's slow progress – though in many ways this was all his own fault – and felt that the other Chinese leaders were betraying the revolution – his revolution. He thought he might, once again, organise the masses and lead them to an even greater revolution.

In the early 1960s *Quotations from Chairman Mao* (the Little Red Book) became the subject of studies for the troops of the People's Liberation Army (PLA) and Mao exhorted the people to learn from the PLA. He was impatient with the Party and the slow pace of change, and, in Beijing, wall posters attacking the university administration began to appear.

Members of the Party were criticised by students, with Mao's approval, and soon the students were issued with red armbands.

To the ordinary Chinese people it all began when the Red Guards swiftly appeared in high schools and colleges and spread like a forest fire leaving a trail of violence and destruction in their wake. Their targets were those in authority – in the Party, in the government, in education, in industry and throughout society as a whole. All in the name of Mao Zedong.

But it was not spontaneous. It had been carefully plotted by Kang Sheng, Mao's security chief, who had also built up Mao's library and supplied him with sexual partners over the years and was said to have introduced Jiang Qing, Mao's wife, to him. Kang had organised vast numbers of young students – the self-styled Red Guards – as undercover agents throughout the high schools and universities. When he gave the word they swept into action. He also ordered the police to provide the Red Guards with any necessary information.

By August 1966, the Cultural Revolution had become official. The Central Cultural Revolution Group (which included Jiang Qing) acted as Mao's official mouthpiece. So it was that Mao's order of March 1966

Countryside near the Special Administrative Region border. (Craig)

to 'liberate the little devils' was carried out literally and specifically, so that 'great disorder across the land might lead to great order'. A spokesman at the Ministry of Public Security said, memorably, 'I am not for beating people to death, but when the masses hate the bad elements so deeply that we are unable to stop them, then don't try ...'

Within ten days, one district on Beijing's northern outskirts had a death toll of 300. The oldest 'reactionary' beaten to death was an 80-year-old granny; the youngest a 38-day -old baby. No place in China was secure from Mao's vicious mindless thugs. In Quangai province, an estimated 67,500 were killed. In Mongolia it was hundreds of thousands. Victim numbers have been estimated at up to four million during ten years of madness. And, worst of all, terrible damage was done to the fabric of a society of great antiquity based on courtesy and community.

Beating sessions in Beijing were organised at sports stadiums. The victims were bound hand and foot, dumped on a floodlit stage and, as the audience bayed for blood, Mao's beardless bullies set on them. Thus did Mao Zedong poison a generation of adolescents who might normally have been regarded as the bright hope of their country's future.

Finally, in the autumn of 1967, Mao withdrew official support for the Cultural Revolution and the Red Guards were no longer in control. The PLA were used to restore order and became deeply involved in most government organisations.

CHAPTER 7

TO SHOW THE CHARACTER
OF US CHINESE

On Sunday 25 June 1950, Korean Radio reported an encounter on the 38th parallel, with very heavy fighting. South Koreans were, it said, attacking the north all along the perimeter. Seoul Radio, too, reported fighting but blamed it on the North Koreans. BBC reports were brief.

It sounded serious to Mao Zedong when he was told. Although he had been warning his colleagues that the United States might intervene in Korea, there is considerable evidence that the attack on the 38th Parallel erupted as a surprise to him and that he was deliberately given no advance warning by North Korea. This had serious consequences. China was in the midst of a drastic reduction in the size of the PLA in order to improve its efficiency as a fighting force. Plans were being drafted for two major operations – the invasion of Taiwan and the take-over of Tibet. Both required large numbers of first class troops, and preparations were moving ahead. Thus, it is highly unlikely that Mao, had he been consulted, would have endorsed such a serious military gamble at this moment. It seems, therefore, that Russia and North Korea quite deliberately excluded China from their plans.

Further, astonishingly, Mao behaved as if he were unaware of the Truman-Acheson Declaration of 5 January 1950, which forecast US recognition of the Mao regime and banned military support for Chiang Kaishek. Nor did he seem aware of the 12 January 1950 statement in Washington and that of 15 March in San Francisco, in which Secretary

BW and PLA Honour Guards, Convention Centre. 1997. (Vince Bell)

of State Dean Acheson put both Korea and Taiwan beyond the US defence perimeter, the capture of the latter being the infant republic's number one priority. This seeming ignorance had serious long-term repercussions for China.

Stalin, however, felt that if he could pick up South Korea without cost, his stranglehold on China, with Outer Mongolia occupied and Russian bases in Manchuria, would be in place. And if China were to receive a bloody nose in the process, so much the better for Stalin. Neither Beijing nor Washington ever understood the real Soviet position at the outbreak of the Korean War. To Washington it looked exactly like a Chinese move. Truman even asked Stalin to intervene with China to help halt the North Koreans.

Mao immediately cancelled demobilisation and ordered the formation of a special north-east Army Group (The 13th), and much toing and froing between Pyongyang, Moscow and Beijing ensued. He also called a meeting to discuss the PLA, domestic problems and the Korean situation. The PLA's worst deficiencies were in the air, but much of its total hardware was of Second World War vintage and worn out. The Chinese People's Republic had been established only ten months earlier and there was so much to be done. As to Korea, that was surely Russia's responsibility. To a man the generals were against sending troops. 'If we're not ready to invade Taiwan,' said one, 'we'd be stupid to think of Korea.'

Mao waited, even after the US General MacArthur landed at Inchon, on 15 September, and began driving the North Koreans back northwards. The 13th Army Group had been ordered to move into positions along the Yalu River, where it awaited orders. Finally, against all military advice, Mao approved the sending of Chinese forces into Korea, as 'a volunteer army', and Stalin agreed to provide air cover and supplies.

However, at the eleventh hour, the Russians informed Zhou Enlai, the Chinese Foreign Minister, that Moscow could not send Soviet air units to Korea, as Stalin had promised, 'because the Soviet forces were not yet properly prepared'. Although this was a staggering blow, Mao decided to go ahead 'to show the character of us Chinese'. They were to have between 450,000 and 500,000 casualties. Lacking artillery, and without anti-aircraft protection the Chinese forces again and again used 'human wave' tactics to try to overwhelm their enemies. But by the time the war had slowed down in 1952, China had paid a price that could not easily be made good. They had fought the US to a standstill but the toll in lives, top divisions, commanders and equipment was staggering. Nor was that the only price Mao paid for joining the North Koreans. The invasion of Taiwan, his priority target in 1949, had to be postponed – as it still is – as that island had meanwhile become a full US ally.

Further, a strict trade embargo was imposed by the United States and its allies which completely froze China out of normal commercial channels and severely hindered its economic development; and diplomatic isolation threw China back onto its reliance on the unloved Soviet Union.

' ... so dear to my heart.'

On 5 February 1952, King George VI died in his sleep. Queen Elizabeth met the blow with her customary courage. Three months later, in May 1952, the 1st Battalion The Black Watch was ordered to Korea. Whenever possible, Queen Elizabeth, as Colonel-in-Chief, had always wished her regiment God-speed before they went on overseas service. Although it was only three months since the death of her husband and she was far from well, Queen Elizabeth – now the Queen Mother – flew from Windsor Castle to Fife to inspect the 1st Battalion at Crail. If she dreaded the duty she never showed it. She wore in her lapel, as she always did when visiting her regiment, the diamond Black Watch Badge presented to her in 1937 by General Sir Archibald Cameron, when she first became the regiment's Colonel-in-Chief, and spoke to them warmly.

> The Black Watch, so dear to my heart and to many of my family who have served with the Regiment, has for more than two hundred years played a distinguished part in the battles of our country. I am proud to think that the traditions which have made you great are cherished and upheld today, and I know well that whatever may face you, you will win new honour for the Black Watch and for Scotland.

Colonel David Rose, the commanding officer, replied: 'We do not know what lies ahead, but I can assure Your Majesty that we shall do everything to uphold the great traditions of Your Majesty's Regiment.'

The 1st Battalion arrived in Korea in July 1952 as part of the Commonwealth Brigade in the United Nations Force and first saw the Hook where they were later to fight their famous battles in the following August. Shaped like a camel's hump, it ran north and south, with smaller ridges running northwards down towards the Chinese lines and, unlike most of the neighbouring hills, was bare of vegetation.

Their first spell in the line lasted a month. The battalion was shelled and heavy rain turned the dusty earth to a morass. There were casualties, but it was really just the *hors d'oeuvre* to what was to come. Colonel Rose writes in his book, *Off the Record – the Life and Letters of a Black Watch Officer*:

> All continues to go well but we are going through an unpleasant time – a few casualties every day. M's Company are getting the worst of it ... really very unpleasant ... we have started to get one or two cases of nerves and shell-shock – the weaker links, of course. It isn't really bad but in this country we are forced to be very concentrated on the hill tops, which makes shelling most unpleasant.

Colonel Rose was consistently inventive, thinking up and introducing new ways to make the Jocks more comfortable. For example, as there appeared to be no threat of attack by the Chinese during daylight hours, he made the forward company 'thin out', removing about 30 men to the back areas for rest and washing. 'No one seems to have thought of this before.'

On 22 July 1952 he wrote:

> It has been pouring with rain all day, with heavy thunderstorms. It's very warm, so one just splashes about in the wet, and everyone is busy trying to keep the ditches open and the water from flooding their dugouts. The roofs are all leaking, my papers are all wet, everything is a thorough mess.

During this period, to keep numbers to the required level, much of the British army was made up of soldiers conscripted for National Service and regulars were, at first, uneasy over what this dilution (in peace time) might do to regimental morale. In the case of the Black Watch, a combination of Colonel Rose's feisty leadership and the Jocks' keen sense of the absurd seemed to do the trick. The battalion all used to wash publicly in the river whenever they could or else right in the open on

Colonel David Rose, CO of 1st Battalion, BW in Korea, examines first photographs of 30 June parade with co-author. (Craig)

their positions. One day, an officer became a bit annoyed because a Jock just stood in front of him and stared. After a while he said, rather testily: 'Have you never seen a cock before?' To which the Jock replied: 'Aye, Sir, plenty. But never a commissioned one.'

By 7 November 1952 the Black Watch were established on the Hook, having taken over from the US Marines. Colonel Rose had watched the Marines' battle on the Hook for several days.

It was an awesome sight. The whole feature was covered most of the time by a cloud of cordite … I had never seen anything like it before … What was I going to do the first night? Had the Chinese suffered enough or would they persevere….? What was to be *my* plan for the Hook position?

He said to the Corps Commander:

Sir, you can't bomb the Chinese out of their tunnels. I am going to dig tunnels. There is nothing left of the old fortifications. We'll start from scratch … I want Korean labour and our sappers. If my men are to fight after several days of bombardment, they must be able to sleep. If the Chinese attack in great numbers, I must be able to use artillery on our own position, then mop up. We can do this if we have tunnels.

The Corps Commander agreed to the plan, telling the colonel that he should come to him direct if he encountered any difficulties.

Colonel Rose was determined that 'his' battle was not going to be a re-run of the last US Marines' affair because the casualties incurred in their counter-attacks were very high. He had made a study of every Chinese attack or raid that he could find out about. The results of their massive bombardments were always the same. Land lines were cut, wireless aerials were shot away. No one knew what was happening for at least an hour. Command Control was always stunned. He was determined to overcome this problem and developed a communication system based on ground aerials. This, of course, reduced the range of sets available, but that problem was overcome by issuing more sets. It was vital to know what was happening at the sharp end so that action could be taken to contain an attack or to mount counter-attacks. Which, of course, was why he was able to react to events so quickly.

As the Black Watch battle developed he realised he was in a very strong position. His communication radio network was extremely effective and so he knew what every section was doing and how they were responding to their Company Commander's orders. As he explained in his book:

> We must hold every dugout, every tunnel. We would reinforce when we could: we would fight each trench and counter-attack if only for 50 yards. At all costs we must hold. Better to hold what we knew we had, than to counter-attack into the unknown.

And that was how the battle developed. The Chinese were milling around everywhere.

> I had given them several doses of 'Air Burst' but there was quite a lot of hand-to-hand fighting ... We were all keyed up to a high pitch but well under control. My Support Company CO was firing incredible quantities of mortar bombs...

Nonetheless they had some anxious moments during the night. Colonel Rose's reserves were all used up so it just remained for the Jocks to slog it out and make sure the Chinese were unable to reinforce the Hook. They now knew most of the routes they used and the likely Forming Up Points. They used every trick in the Gunners' book – star shells, random 'stonks' – and it worked. The Chinese were 'getting that dreadful thing, shell fire when you are in the open and on the move. Our last job was to cut off those Chinese who were still on the Hook, as they went away with their dead and wounded.' The Chinese were meticulous about this.

In a letter, Colonel Rose summed up:

BW Visitors' Book,
entries written after
Beating Retreat and
Dinner with the PLA.

(Craig)

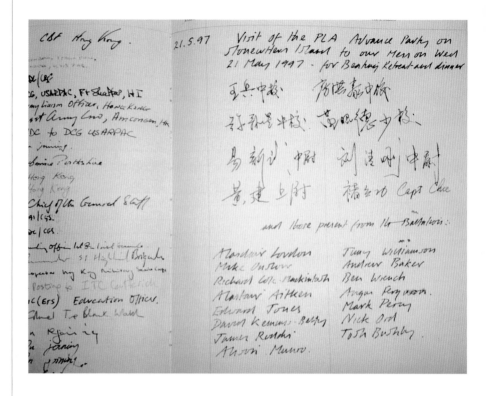

The men are very proud of themselves and rightly so. Every officer and man did his stuff – no heroics but damned well and efficiently. It shook the Chinks good and proper.

The Black Watch had four officers wounded, one killed. There were 16 men missing, ten dead, 60 or 70 wounded, many not badly. This battle has been described as 'a classic of its kind and size'.

The Korean war in 1952–53 was a night war and as Colonel Rose points out:

that was to our disadvantage, with our semi-trained troops. That was our only disadvantage. I think we should have made more use of Artificial Moonlight (search lights reflected off the clouds). We had the generating capacity and the communications to switch on and off at will. If you can see the battlefield, you need not use thousands of shells and mortar bombs on Defensive Fire.

He thought the Chinese were very good at night, very fast moving and very quick to react with their weapons. They did not attack during full moons but were constantly probing at other times, digging caves etc which could be used as Forming Up Points or as Advanced Dressing Stations. Their fortitude, he says, in the face of complete domination with all weapons, was truly staggering.

The Colonel in Chief meets the next generation, Fort George, Inverness. (Frank Proctor)

CHAPTER 8

THE DRAGON STRIKES

By 1971, Mao realised that his dream of transforming China by launching its youth against his own party in the name of 'great democracy' had turned into an appalling catastrophe and, once again, he turned to Deng Xiaoping and Prime Minister Zhou Enlai to drag the country back from disaster.

Deng had been toppled from the leadership as a 'capitalist roader' but Mao seems to have had a grudging affection for the man who stubbornly defied him. He had merely been expelled to a small town and his family allowed to join him. This, of course, was also Prime Minister Zhou Enlai's doing. He stayed in the group around Mao, the better to thwart their plans for a takeover and to safeguard as many intellectuals as he could, as well as party members. So, in April 1973, Deng Xiaoping reappeared in public at a state banquet and later he was in New York at the United Nations. By 1975, he was doing most of the work for the desperately ill Prime Minister.

During the last months of Zhou Enlai's life, the battle between him and the faction around Jiang Qing, later to be called the Gang of Four, burst into the open. When he died, after 14 operations during which cancer was found in every organ in his body, great demonstrations took place in Tiananmen Square. The Gang of Four called these gatherings 'counter-revolutionary', and Deng Xiaoping was accused of having organised them. He was arrested but, once again, Mao had his way and he was allowed to leave for Guangdong province, in South China, where he was protected by an important army commander, Marshal Ye Jianying. However, his drive for change came to a halt. He had raised the gross output of industry and agriculture, railways were running, farmers had gone back to the fields and factories were back in production. Education was still in a mess but the foundations were laid.

But Mao still did not trust Jiang Qing or her associates and elevated Hua Guofeng, a fifth ranking vice-premier, to be acting premier. Deng was out – or worse. However, the Gang of Four's constant stream of abuse against him drummed up public support. If he was so bad in the Gang's eyes, he must be very good.

On 9 September 1976 Mao Zedong died, the Gang of Four were arrested and Deng Xiaoping could return to centre stage. He had a solid phalanx of supporters within the Party, especially all the Long Marchers, because he was of the same generation as Mao Zedong and Zhou Enlai, the generation that had created the history of contemporary China. They had built the Communist Party, fought the Japanese, fought the Nationalist Chiang Kaishek and established the People's Republic of China in 1949. And despite Mao's attempts, they had survived and were back and Deng Xiaoping was one of them. Thus China was again ruled by the original Communists, all in their eighties now. And there, maybe, lay the root cause of Tiananmen Square.

Only people in the deep countryside could judge the power of the revolution that Deng Xiaoping set off in the villages where 80 per cent of the Chinese people still lived. He quietly gave the land back to the peasants, demolished the communes and put money back into people's pockets, money they had earned themselves. They could divide the land as they pleased and plant what they wanted and the countryside began to blossom as never before. And it was all done without propaganda or sterile slogans. Deng promised there would be no more hysterical campaigns, no more model farms, model factories, model soldiers, model workmen, model peasants and no more theoretical economy. For the peasants it was a wonderful time.

Then some of the old Party leaders began to be uneasy at the speed

Fruit market, Diamond Hill, Kowloon. (Craig)

and pragmatism of Deng's reforms. They preferred a slower rate of change and when they felt his free-wheeling policies were wavering out of control, they attacked Hu Yaobang, his Party deputy. They did not attack Deng's policies directly because they were working; but they were also stimulating inflation, increasing prices and making many items scarce. They were concerned about what exactly was going on in the new trade zones. Were they becoming hotbeds of immorality and corruption – typical of capitalism?

Unfortunately, their disquiet coincided with more student protest, which Deng ordered Hu Yaobang to deal with. This he did, and again in 1986 and 1987. However, these student disorders irritated the old guard even more than Deng's policies and they again moved against Hu Yaobang because, they said, he and his associates were spreading unconventional ideas that were inflaming the students. It was time for a return to conventional Communism and Marxist economics.

Finally, when the students began marching with banners demanding democracy, the two sides could agree at last, and Deng fired Hu Yaobang, replacing him with Zhao Ziyang, who was regarded as sound. This move did not solve his problems but did allow a brief period of comparative quiet.

Tensions began to rise again in the spring of 1988 over the economic programme, about inflation in the cities and price rises in basic goods in the countryside. Despite this public unrest, it became clear at the annual June gathering of Party leaders at the seaside resort of Beidaihe that Deng was determined to continue his policies. This greatly alarmed the orthodox, and in the end they clipped his wings by handing over all economic matters to Premier Li Peng. All summer, rumours circulated in Beijing and were spread abroad by diplomats. China was in a shambles, and Deng was finished.

Then Chinese Central Television showed a dramatic six-episode documentary called *The Yellow River Elegy*. This was seen by an estimated 70 million viewers, and many more watched the re-run. Why was this film so explosive? It attacked the foundations of Chinese belief. For centuries the Chinese have proudly described themselves as the Yellow River civilisation. On that great and dangerous river China had been born.

The documentary blamed the river and its worship for China's failure to enter the modern world. While the British, the Italians, the Spaniards and the Portuguese were sailing the seas and discovering new countries and their riches, the Chinese had hardly ventured out of sight of land. They had built a vast empire, but by the 14th Century it was hopelessly out of date. The film also mocked beliefs about the Great Wall, which cost billions in treasure and millions in lives. It was built to keep the barbarians out but never did. It merely, said the documentary, kept the Chinese in. They did not travel abroad to strange lands, as Europeans did; they stayed at home. They walled their cities, their homes and their minds.

The dragon, too, as the symbol of the all-powerful emperor, had held the country back. There could be only one 'dragon' so that whilst this legend held sway, China could not enter the modern world with, say, a parliamentary system with a free-speaking electorate.

Nothing more daring or controversial than this documentary could have been shown, and it became obvious that eventually there would have to be a showdown and that Deng would fight his corner in the old way – the dragon way.

Meanwhile, attention turned to the visit planned by President Gorbachev in May 1989. Everyone hoped that 20 years of hostilities would end in a triumph for Deng. The Russians were seriously interested in China's policies, and it is tempting to speculate what might have been – given what later happened in China and Russia – if the summit had gone according to plan. Each leader wanted change and reform. Perhaps Tiananmen Square's least publicised but most serious blow was to their converging visions of the future.

In April 1989, Hu Yaobang died of a heart attack and everything changed. Overnight he became the student's hero. It was not at first apparent to either party that a major confrontation was in the offing. The students at the start were concerned with their own problems – bad food, lousy dormitory conditions and a lack of financial support. But they also wanted justice for Hu Yaobang and a full and honourable funeral, though the latter got lost somewhere in the confusion as the crowds grew.

The memorial service for Hu Yaobang was held in the Great Hall of the People on Saturday 22 April. To outflank the students it was announced that Tiananmen Square would be closed on the day of the ceremony, but they pre-empted this by arriving the night before.

Where would it all end? The students were split. Many saw no reason to go on after the funeral. They had made their point. The government seemed inclined to think that discussions would demonstrate weakness. It was an intractable problem and required decisive but sensitive action. So the days dragged on with the government denouncing the students as anti-Party, anti-government and planning 'conspiracy and turmoil' – evoking ghastly memories of Mao's Cultural Revolution – whilst the students, who now were in the main patriotic and idealistic, turned up in even greater numbers, greatly alarming the old guard who had all faced Red Guard masses under Mao – at some personal cost.

Nevertheless, Zhao Ziyang told his propaganda chiefs to take a more conciliatory stance on reporting the students. However, these orders coincided with a huge influx of international press and TV reporters covering the Deng-Gorbachev talks, who soon flooded the world with reports about the students. China was suddenly exposed as never before. It is not clear whether Deng and the old guard ever really appreciated this fact, even when the images of firing tanks flashed around the globe.

Thus matters rolled along with suspicion, indecision and misunderstanding on both sides as the pace quickened. One million people had filled the square the day before President Gorbachev left for Shanghai and by now Beijingers had taken the students to their hearts. It was extraordinary: hundreds of thousands parading in the square, housewives carrying food, medical teams arriving to care for the hunger strikers, government workers carrying banners inscribed with the names of their departments, young television employees chanting 'We tell lies. Don't believe us'. The atmosphere was friendly and excited.

There were one or two chances to avoid the final bloody outcome. For instance, on the day when Li Peng and Zhao Ziyang met students in the Great Hall and the Square on 19 May – Zhao's last public appearance. The students, at a low ebb themselves, saw the split between the two officials and, that evening, called off their hunger strike. Had

Detail of Pillar of Shame, Victoria Park. Hong Kong 1997. (Craig)

somebody seized that moment, the demonstration could well have soon been over. But nobody reacted.

Nevertheless, by the weekend of 27 – 28 May, enthusiasm was diminishing anyway and students were drifting back home. Many of their leaders felt the demonstration had served its purpose and were deciding to leave, offering another opportunity for peaceful settlement. But by now it seemed that Deng was determined to 'spill some blood' and teach the students a lesson. On the evening of 30 May, the statue of the Goddess of Democracy was brought and was put up in Tiananmen Square directly in front of the portrait of Mao. This was the students' last move. If this did not bring back the crowds, the whole thing would have to be called off. Thousands of Beijingers flocked back to the square. The TV cameras, of course, loved every minute but it probably proved the last straw for the old guard. Minds were made up.

So, the Goddess statue did provide a temporary boost but, nonetheless, the number of protesters continued to fall. On 2 June, the square was half-deserted by late afternoon, and Deng Xiaoping made his decision. To him it seemed the people were threatening the Communist state. The 27th and 38th Armies of the PLA would move towards Tiananmen Square.

Tiananmen Square Memorial meeting, 4 June 1997. (Craig)

There are three significant factors to consider.

1. With so many camera crews *in situ* there was great danger, as time passed, that the medium was becoming the message. The seduction of the camera is well-known. Very few can resist its blandishments. And some of the student leaders were rather obvious news fodder.

2. On 30 May, a Hong Kong support group arrived with $US 650,000 and $HK 2,000,000 for the students. What effect did this have in bolstering the demonstrators' resolve (to their ultimate detriment) and is there not some justification for China's suspicions that Hong Kong was a hotbed of irresponsible intrigue?

3. The high casualties. 1,000–2,000 killed in Beijing, 300 of them around Tiananmen Square, is the best estimate. This is not the place for a detailed description of the final horror about which, as ever, there are differing versions: some say that many were killed in the square, others that no one at all was killed there. It may be that, strictly speaking, the first report is correct, but deaths certainly occurred in adjacent areas.

Handover Dragon, Tsim
Tsa Tsui. 1997. (Craig)

What is certain is that warnings were broadcast for two hours (from 1800 hrs) that people should clear the streets and go home, because action was going to be taken. Why did so few heed these warnings? Many think it was because no one really believed that the People's Liberation Army would *actually* do the unthinkable and shoot.

CHAPTER 9

EVERYTHING THAT WE DO
WILL BE HIGH PROFILE

No one should doubt the significance of 30 June 1997. The handover
of the Sovereignty of Hong Kong to China is a huge event in China,
with every school in the land counting the days until the dreadful
wrong of British rule is ended. In the West the handover of the last
British colony is also of huge significance. I state this because it affects
1 Black Watch in two main ways: first, we are extremely fortunate to
be in Hong Kong over this period, and to take an intimate part in the
handover itself. Second, everything that we do will be high profile,
and some sections of the press will jump on any minor incident of
ours and build it up as an example of major decadence. We must all
assume that someone will be watching us (usually through a lens)
whatever we are doing.

Lieutenant Colonel Alasdair Loudon,
Commanding Officer 1BW, 23 January 1997

The Black Watch had been *in situ* since February 1997 and already knew
how perceptive those words were.

In 1992 it was decided that, as all parties genuinely wanted a smooth
transfer of power, it was possible to reduce the size of the Hong Kong
garrison, with benefits for both Hong Kong and British defence
expenditure. So it was scaled down from 9,500 to 3,250 during 1994 – a
reduction of two thirds within 12 months and an amazing achievement

at short notice. The garrison stayed at that strength until August 1996 when, between then and March 1997 most British and Nepali families finally returned to the UK.

It was an unusual garrison *vis-à-vis* the British armed forces, because it was both tri-service – Royal Navy, Army and Royal Air Force – and tri-national – British, Gurkha and Hong Kong Chinese. It was also the second oldest remaining British garrison, only Gibraltar is older.

By the end of April 1997 this 'draw down' – the reduction of men and materials to be ready for the 30 June handover – was nearly completed. The British Military Hospital at King's Park, Kowloon which, in its 28 years of operation, had treated more than 150,000 in-patients and delivered some 50,000 babies, had been closed in 1995. The Royal Hong Kong Regiment (The Volunteers) had been disbanded in September 1995. During the Second World War, they had been awarded 19 decorations and 18 mentions in dispatches from a strength of only 2,200 men. After 54 years service, there was sadness that none were awarded a British passport.

The 1st Battalion of the Royal Gurkha Rifles had left for the UK in October 1996 – their departure marking the end of 40 years' continuous service by Gurkha Infantrymen in Hong Kong – leaving only the Gurkha Signals, whilst the Royal Navy LEP (Locally Enlisted Personnel) held its

Pipe Major, Royal Gurkha Regiment, rehearsing his Pipes and Drums, 1997. (Craig)

final division on 6 December 1996. The Royal Hong Kong Squadron remained on duty until 30 June 1997, as did the RAF No 28 (AC) Squadron.

The garrison strength at the end of May had fallen to 1,600, leaving only the garrison's operational elements which were to be withdrawn in the final weeks before the handover. The Black Watch (RHR) HQ and half the battalion were based on Stonecutters' Island. Additionally, there was one company based at Osborn Barracks and one in a training camp at High Island. Thus, The Prince of Wales Barracks, which condenses into less than half a hectare, departments and facilities which, in the old Victoria Barracks, spread over 19 hectares, added a valuable dimension to our activities. We began to home in on it for a variety of purposes.

We had visited Fort George (The Regimental Depot) and Perth earlier in the year to make working contact with the battalion and had played hide-and-seek with them at Heathrow – experiencing the vagaries of air travel – as they flew out to Hong Kong in their different groups. But we had not really seen them at work. So it was with a mixture of keen anticipation and mild apprehension that I waited for the CO's car beside the tower opposite the Cultural Centre, Kowloon. Keen anticipation because, during our initial two weeks getting to know some of the ins and outs of Hong Kong, we had seen the odd flash of a red hackle and the adrenalin had started to flow and mild apprehension because you can never go back.

My driver proved an entertaining and informative companion remarking, with a grin, as I received (or rather the CO's car did) a crisp salute from the Main Gate sentry, 'I'll bet that gave your ego a wee boost, Sir'. And then I was meeting the Adjutant, the CO, Colonel Loudon, and others in the ante-room as we moved to the dining room for lunch. In his Hong Kong Training Directive, issued on 23 January 1997, the CO had decreed that communication with the press should be open policy, but within reason. So as people talked, I tried to explain how we were setting about writing this book and to make the vital distinction between the press and us.

Colonel Loudon arranged for us to have day passes for the entire period up to the last three days, both to Stonecutters' Island and to Prince of Wales Barracks (POWB), and this included use of the launches that plied between the two military bases. This enabled us to come and go at will and unaccompanied because we soon got generally known. However, there was constant vigilance, and our activities were always noted.

We became familiar, for instance, with a smart Chinese (British Forces) Military Policeman who seemed omnipresent, though not always in uniform. Whatever we did, together or apart, in POWB, he would appear, sometimes looking very relaxed in shorts as if straight from the swimming pool. He moved like a wraith and whenever we met there was always a slightly sinister smile of recognition. Our last glimpse of him was on Handover Day as we sat by the swimming pool watching groups of Chinese kitchen and cleaning staff saying their last goodbyes – he suddenly materialised from behind the NAAFI counter, clutching a huge mug of tea and gave us a last quizzical glance.

The NAAFI, in many ways the hub of the barracks, in buildings adjacent to the most valuable swimming pool in the world – with land values at around HK$1 million per square metre it is worth around HK$350,000,000 (£2.92 million) – constantly supplied delicious meals, both English and Chinese, and, of course, large mugs of invigorating tea. It was a perfect place to meet people, rest, regroup, write up notes or just watch the garrison world go by. Nearby shops included the NAAFI

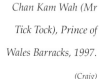

Chan Kam Wah (Mr Tick Tock), Prince of Wales Barracks, 1997.

(Craig)

store, a barber, a photographer, a Chinese artefact shop, a Forces Post Office, a splendid military tailors, a watch and jewellery shop (Mr Tick Tok) and, set apart, the dental surgery.

Parallel to the waterfront, in this same area, is Blake Block where, during the last weeks of June, an Advance Guard of the People's Liberation Army stayed and were occasionally sighted, though they kept very much to themselves.

The main tower – 27 floors with the Gurkha Signals Radar Facilities on the roof – was another favourite haunt. From a variety of heights we could see what was going on at all points of the compass. To the south one could see Government House, home of Governor Patten – though not for long, and to the north all the craft moving up and down one of the busiest waterways in the world, the helicopters chopping in and out and HMS *Chatham* berthed far below. There were pot plants around a tiled portion of the top roof and a solitary deck chair for whoever was on duty – or off duty.

Or one could look eastwards to the extension to the Convention Centre, with small, crawling figures on its roof-top working right up to the last day to make it ready for the Handover Ceremony that would initiate its use.

On the Star Ferry coming into Wanchai, on our first day, we had seen these tiny figures, from below, crawling around on an amazing network of bamboo scaffolding and all over the roof. Later that month they were to complain that the subcontractor was not paying their wages and that the lack of toilet facilities at the top was a great nuisance.

Still looking east, immediately below, one could see the yellow hard hats of the Chinese working on the road between HQBF and East Tamar, the original naval basin now filled in and set aside for the final Farewell Parade, where metal stands, tents, temporary toilets and camera towers were being set up. During the last days large, hollow plastic barricades (like central heating radiators) were brought in and piled to one side. Light when empty, they are formidable obstacles when filled with water.

The estimated £3 billion real-estate value of the parade ground probably makes it the most expensive in the world. It will be used once

*Press as HMY
Britannia arrives at
Hong Kong. June 1997.*

(Craig)

only, and will certainly be a spectacular swan-song to the career of Garrison Sergeant Major WO1 Vince Bell, Coldstream Guards, the man responsible for the military elements of the Handover ceremonies. No stranger to the job, he's been organising parades since 1989 including Trooping the Colour, the 50th anniversary HK Liberation Day, the disbandment parades for the Queen's Gurkha Engineers, the Hong Kong Military Service Corps, the closure of RAF Sek Kong and the departure of the 1st Bn. Royal Gurkha Rifles. Each occasion has been used to try out ideas for the final parade.

There is a scale model of the parade ground on his office wall with

*HMS Chatham at still
unfinished quayside
with Convention Centre
in background. June
1997. (Craig)*

paper cut-outs representing the numbers who will be there in the various guards and bands.

'It's accurate to the last centimetre,' he says, 'I need to know exactly how much space I have to ensure that the movements I've included are possible. The trick is to make the parade as spectacular as possible but keeping it as simple as I can, bearing in mind we'll only have two weeks for rehearsal.'

He would have liked longer, he said, pointing out that rehearsals for Trooping the Colour begin two months beforehand. Nevertheless, he's confident the parade will be up to his demanding standards, and at midnight on 30 June, after 25 years' service, WO1 Vince Bell will retire ('unwillingly') from the army.

From here, too, one could see helicopters flying in and out from the landing pads on the harbour front just beyond where the Royal Yacht *Britannia* would berth. One week before the handover, having first escorted her in on a press launch, we nipped up to the sixth floor and photographed her berthing and the press queuing nearby. A couple of weeks previously we had also seen HMS *Chatham* berthing beside the still unfinished infilled waterfront. Her arrival underlined the last run-in to the handover and signalled a general increase in the tempo of life.

North across the harbour lay Kowloon and its background hills and, again, below the tower, a new road in the making, running from east to west alongside the harbour, which during the last month had been turned from rubble into its final asphalt surface, on the sea side of which green grass miraculously appeared just in time for the handover. Chinese workmen, their hard hats sticking through their bamboo sun hats, worked round the clock to finish the job exactly on time. There were high policy and financial reasons for these niceties. At times, the combination of noise, heat and dust was oppressive but the workmen managed to stay cheerful and undaunted. From the 27th floor there is access to the roof and, by way of a fixed ladder, further access to the Gurkha Signals radar platform. We sought out the last Officer Commanding Hong Kong Gurkha Signals Squadron, Major Tim Craven, who had invited us to see it all as it was about to be dismantled; it would all be gone well before the PLA arrived. They were a lively group. Earlier in the day they had paraded for an Italian TV Unit whose director turned up very late. Major Craven's comments to the cameraman about timing and professionalism were memorably succinct. Then the errant director asked the Gurkhas, from the Queen's Gurkha Signals Squadron, 'to march about and do kukri drill'.

'But we are Gurkha Signals,' said Captain Navindra Gurung, with the look on his face of a man fighting a lost cause; 'We do not do kukri drill'. However, the Italians had their requirements so the Gurkhas had a quick consultation, smiled a lot, flashed their kukris around and then put on a perfect little display of marching and kukri drill for the delighted film crew. The Gurkhas' thoughts could not have been half as pleasant as their demeanour.

Below the radar platform were several floors of barrack rooms, each with an enormous mirror adjacent to the exit for fine checking of turnout and facilities including a large gym and the Gurkhas' administrative offices. A few signalmen would remain for the handover in case of typhoon emergencies. On the 26th floor was the Officers' Mess, which had magnificent views across the harbour to Kowloon and the hills, west towards Macau and east to the Lei Yue Mun straits. This housed the capacious mess in which the Black Watch and Gurkha Pipes and Drums, and others, were to wait for hours on 30 June, in full ceremonial dress, after crossing from Stonecutters' Island, until they stepped out to thunderous applause onto the farewell parade ground. The space and air-conditioning would prove essential in the humidity and tension.

As the garrison was already much reduced and everyone left was very busy with rehearsals or administrative tidying up, this pleasant room was often nearly empty and although the furniture and fittings were eye-catching, it looked distinctly odd to see white plastic cutlery – replacing the already packed silver – laid on the richly glowing tables. All the furniture had been auctioned and nothing at all would be left for the incomers – least of all the large portrait of The Queen, for if it was, it would become the property of the Hong Kong government which would then, *ipso facto*, have to maintain it. This was not the arrangement.

CHAPTER 10

TODAY WANG DAN,
TOMORROW YOU AND ME

In the end, history will judge Hong Kong's transfer of sovereignty not by fireworks, dignitaries or the grandeur of the handover ceremony, but by the institutions left behind to enable us to preserve Hong Kong's rule of law and way of life.

Martin Lee. *The Daily Telegraph*. 23 October 1996.

Lawyer Martin Lee in his Chambers. (Craig)

On 4 June, as Hong Kong prepared for a huge demonstration on the 8th anniversary of Tiananmen Square, we talked in his Chambers to Martin Lee, Chairman of the Democratic Party and Hong Kong's most influential legislator, appointed Queen's Counsel in 1979, and Chairman of the Hong Kong Bar Association 1980–83. His party had won 85 per cent of the votes in the 1995 elections to the Legislative Council, but that legislature, elected for a four year term would be abolished on 1 July and replaced by a Beijing-appointed body, 'the Provisional Legislature'.

We were fortunate to talk to Martin Lee and pleased to be supplied with a sheaf of photocopied articles written by him, although there was no time to peruse them before we met in his book-lined, comfortable Chambers and seated ourselves at the round, well-polished table. These articles spell out the fears and perplexities of the Hong Kong people at this important moment in their history and written by the leader of Hong Kong's most popular political Party, they help not only to clarify why so many (though, of course, not all) feared reunification with China but also why the imminent arrival of 4,000 PLA troops, the Tiananmen Square army which had repressed the protesters so brutally, was causing so much consternation.

'People are prepared to criticise the British government and Patten, but China – no!' Martin Lee spoke of a national tendency to temper protest as oppression becomes more severe and because China already had 'all the buttons set up': China would control the executive and had already appointed the first Chief Executive, Tung Chee Hwa; had already appointed the Provisional Legislature; it would control the Courts, and the new Court of Final Appeal would not be allowed to interpret key articles of the Basic Law – 'the highest court shall have "no jurisdiction over acts of state, such as defence, foreign affairs, etcetera". It is this etcetera that is worrying here ... as it should be to the people throughout Asia who do business in Hong Kong'.

Martin Lee had pointed out that text books were being changed – (well, they are always being changed but not, as now, by the Foreign Minister of China!) – that universities in Hong Kong already had Vice-Chancellors appointed by China; and that in the press self-censorship had already begun. Hong Kong had been promised a 'hands-off' policy but China was, in fact, demonstrating a 'hands-on' policy. What then was the best scenario for Hong Kong? 'That the buttons are not pressed.'

We asked him about 'the unholy alliance', Hong Kong's capitalists and China's Communists? 'Ah, the fat cats tangoing with the Communists, cheek to cheek'. Freedom would be sacrificed to prosperity, he said; the poor people would be the ones to suffer most and the have-nots would be even more deprived; control was good for business, and demonstrators made for instability. Tung, the designated new Chief

Executive, was, he believed, a good man, sincere, genuine.

> But I would not force my values on others who had not elected me.
> Tung brags about 'Chinese values' and he can only properly impose
> those values if he put them in a policy statement upon which he has
> been elected. His Chinese values are old-fashioned, two generations
> out of line with the Hong Kong people; he has no mandate from the
> people he governs and he was chosen by 400 men and women,
> themselves appointed to the task by Beijing ... Beijing on the surface
> is calm – but how long for?

Martin Lee is prized not only in Hong Kong but also on the world stage.
In June 1995 *Asiaweek* magazine named him one of 'Twenty Great Asians'
who had changed the region over the past 20 years; in March 1996,
Liberal International awarded him the Prize for Freedom at the World
Council of Liberals' meeting in Edinburgh; and in April 1997, the
National Endowment for Democracy presented him with its 1997
Democracy Award on Capitol Hill.

 On 6 November 1996, writing in the *South China Morning Post*, Martin
Lee illustrated fears about threats to Hong Kong citizens' long-enjoyed
freedom of expression: 'As we debate the motion on Wang Dan in the
Legislative Council this afternoon, I will think of one thing: today, Wang
Dan; tomorrow, you and me.'

The previous week, Wang Dan, a 27-year-old former student leader
had been jailed for 11 years by the Chinese authorities and officially
convicted of plotting to subvert the government, in Lee's words,
'sentenced for doing something we do every day in Hong Kong – writing
articles in newspapers'. He went on:

> Could Wang's fate befall any of us in Hong Kong? After 1 July 1997
> the Beijing appointed legislature will pass a law against 'subversion',
> which is a Communist concept, a concept that runs contrary to and
> is alien to Hong Kong's common law and courts.

But despite Martin Lee's conviction that Beijing in 1997 sought to have the mechanism to control Hong Kong any time it wished, it might not indeed take control, all might not be lost, if the Hong Kong people stood up for their freedom and the international community supported them, especially 'the United States, as the standard-bearer of world democracy and England, our colonial ruler'. This would be the best hope for China's own efforts to establish a visible legal system and a rule of law.

Martin Lee told us that Mrs Thatcher had acknowledged a moral obligation to monitor, and to stand up for, Hong Kong's rights but there was a legal obligation too. We asked what the new Prime Minister, Tony Blair, could do for Hong Kong? He said he should come to Hong Kong for the handover ceremony, he should tell the whole world the Provisional Legislature is unconstitutional and he should not attend the ceremony which was to take place almost immediately after the handover ceremony to swear in its members. (In fact, Blair did attend the first ceremony but did not attend the second.) The new Labour government was in a better position than the Conservatives to do something for Hong Kong, since human rights were high on its agenda; it had a large parliamentary majority and an improved relationship with

Discussion group at Tiananmen Memorial meeting, Victoria Park. 1997. (Craig)

China and would not be as influenced by big business as the Conservatives had been. He hoped the Labour government would take positive action.

Martin Lee's dream?

I don't have a dream but something more positive – a vision for China, my country, China, that it will become a really great nation in which the human rights of every citizen will be protected by Chinese law. Then we can hold our heads high.

We overran our allotted time but there had been no hint that we should leave. We went down the lift from Lee's Chambers in Admiralty Centre, preparing to move on to the demonstration in Victoria Park. There was a pat on the shoulder as we moved through the lunch-time throng and, looking round, we saw Martin Lee disappearing quickly into the crowd.

CHAPTER 11

A PARTY-ARMY WITH
PROFESSIONAL CHARACTERISTICS

The People's Liberation Army, as represented by the immaculate soldiers crossing the rain-lashed Hong Kong border at Lok Ma Chau on 1 July 1997 as compared with those deemed 'too poor and scruffy-looking to have defeated the Japanese' by the citizens of Jinzhou, Manchuria in 1945, has travelled a long road and is still on that journey. There is no doubt that, as with the rest of China, the PLA is in transition, and that the servicemen to be seen in Hong Kong represented the Chinese military – the Army, the Navy and the Air Force all fall under the PLA designation – edging towards the future role it thinks it wants to play. And by so doing it has left little doubt about its pivotal role in the post-Deng Xiaoping era.

The PLA has always been a central force in Chinese politics because of the unique Army/Party relationship that has existed since the very beginnings of the Communist regime in 1949. And although there will obviously be changes they will remain linked to the new leadership of necessity because they comprise the forces by which that leadership can acquire, hold on to and increase power.

However, it is not clear exactly what the PLA's role will be over the next decade because their actions will be partly determined by what happens in the political arena and this is also unclear. Furthermore, some of the factors that have shaped their behaviour hitherto are themselves undergoing change, with effects that are, yet again, unclear. In fact, the

Garrison Sergeant Major meets with his PLA counterpart. 1997.

(Vince Bell)

PLA is a 'Party-Army with professional characteristics'. It is not a professional army in the Western sense because of the way it has developed and the nature of the regime it serves. On the other hand, it is not just Party-fodder because the professionalism of its officers has often made them question and sometimes even refute Party policies which they think are incompatible with their military duty.

After the setting up of the Communist regime in 1949, the distinction between the roles of the top leaders – that is between military and political – was indistinct because most of them had led troops in the revolutionary period and, *ipso facto*, had a hand in setting up the Communist Party. They were an integral part of both institutions so it seemed quite natural for them to cross the boundaries between the two. Thus Mao Zedong and Deng Xiaoping, who had been supreme commanders in the PLA, also became top Party leaders. Their military reputations enabled them both to use the army as their power base in politics; both knew they could always count on the military when push came to shove. And so did others.

Of course, there have been instances of more blatant use such as the

103

Cultural Revolution, the move against the Gang of Four after Mao's death and, most seriously for the PLA, Tiananmen Square. The Fish/Water link idea which was used to demonstrate that the PLA really was the People's Army also illustrates the relationship between that army and its government. Because there has been a Communist government in China since 1949 and therefore there has only been one party, the first duty of the PLA is loyalty to the Communist Party. The Army has been wholly state-funded in the past. However, there are changes occurring which have altered this relationship and which will continue to do so. If being a 'Party-Army with professional characteristics' seems a contradiction in terms, it must be remembered that the PLA has never been used to advance its own interests. It has never moved into politics on its own initiative but only when someone – Mao or Deng – ordered it to do so.

The first serious intervention by the Army was during the Cultural Revolution ostensibly to 'support the left' but in fact to restore order in the chaos created by the Red Guard's destructive excesses. The second occasion was in the Tiananmen Square crisis and was entirely different. This was the regime taking action against its own citizens who it claimed were aiming to overthrow it. The PLA did not interfere in any way or take sides. It was ordered to squash the demonstrators and did so, with some hesitations and misgivings – amply justified by events – and some instances of disobedience. The PLA, in brief, has never been an army seeking political power. Indeed both the above events were opposed by senior commanders who foresaw all the dangers.

With the death of Deng Xiaoping, an entirely new era has dawned. President Jiang Zemin has no military background, nor anything like the same long-standing military networks or personal authority inside the military. And China's requirements are changing. For the first time in some 150 years China faces no serious external military threat. The assumption of an inevitable global war that would pit China against Russia remained constant from the late 1960s to the first half of the 1980s. That threat evaporated in 1985 and a new policy was introduced which required the PLA to change from preparation for 'early war, major war, and nuclear war' to 'peacetime army building'. China has decided that

the danger of a major (US/Russia) war before the year 2000 is almost non-existent, the danger of a medium-scale local war (Taiwan) is possible and small-scale conventional wars (border region incidents) are likely.

In tandem with these military requirements have been Deng's economic changes. He removed Mao's disastrous communes and told the peasants, without a great flurry of trumpets, that to make a profit was a good thing. In fact, he moved swiftly but quietly towards capitalism or, as he called it, 'Socialism with Chinese characteristics'. This, of course, entails a complete restructuring of the whole hitherto state-controlled industrial base, massive unemployment with more and more institutions having to pay their own way and the PLA being reduced from 5,000,000 to 3,000,000 and being told to become entrepreneurial and use its surplus equipment and staff in lieu of a declining budget.

Thus, what has been called 'People's Liberation Army Inc.' invaded the business world. Defence factories changed to the production of civilian goods, five-star PLA hotels sprang up and military units opened joint ventures with foreign concerns. The air force decommissioned planes, pilots and airports for commercial use, the navy opened ports and leased ships for commercial shipping, and the construction corps began building bridges, canals and roads for money whilst the army leased lorries and soldiers for commercial building projects. The PLA admits to having 10,000 companies under its control but some analysts think it could be twice as many.

All this, of course, leads to the possibility of corruption, which is not good for the PLA's state of readiness or its professionalism. For example, undeclared profits are laundered in Hong Kong and then channelled to offshore tax-haven accounts. The police told us of expensive cars being smuggled from Hong Kong to mainland China and one officer said with a laugh, 'just take a look at the number of left-hand drive Mercs (BMWs now) at any big event in Beijing'. Hence the increased politicisation to bring the military under tighter control and the campaigns against corruption.

Another side-effect of all this is that the financial independence of PLA units can make it easier for them to turn a deaf ear to Beijing. If they are running a joint venture with the authority in whose region they are stationed, it gives them common cause against orders from the centre.

It must be emphasised here that there are *many* centres of excellence throughout the PLA, especially in the Officer Corps, which are helping to build up a more professional army, an *esprit de corps* and a sense of historical achievement. This is also part of a new patriotic nationalism which is taking over from the rapidly reducing role of Communism.

Scots Guards bandsmen with their PLA counterparts. 1997.

(David Price)

All agree the Communist Party itself must be modernised, a process which Deng Xiaoping had already begun with his 'Socialism with a modern face' and that the military will help to redefine the legality of the Party which does not preach egalitarianism any more but prosperity and reform – and at different paces. A new and difficult culture for any troops to absorb.

'subtext of tease and tension.'

On the whole, people are more interested in 'baddies' than 'goodies', so it was likely that in the unique situation of the change of sovereignty in Hong Kong, some would not be able to resist the temptation to find a villain. The People's Liberation Army suited the role almost perfectly – they were armed, unfamiliar and above all, imminent. It would be easy to transform these troops into marauding hordes, animals, tanked to the teeth, agents of rape and pillage who would wreak havoc throughout the territory, lock up its defiant citizens, take over its key buildings and communication systems and, amidst rivers of blood, install Beijing as the new masters – especially for those who carried the psychological baggage of those images of Tiananmen Square which were indelibly printed on the imagination.

None of this was articulated, but was planted by innuendo and hint in minds the world over, which for eight years had associated the Chinese army with acts of senseless terror, and especially in Hong Kong where the population, 97 per cent Chinese, knew that those who had ordered these atrocities – or their successors – would become their new masters.

In the days and weeks before the handover, the media could have provided well-researched information about the nature of the PLA in 1997, how it had changed since 1989 (though, in fact, even then the massacre was an act of state, rather than the responsibility of the army), how it wished to become professional, earn respect, and, if it could not eradicate memories of Tiananmen Square, at least perform its duties in such a way as to make a clear distinction in people's minds between the image they held of the army as it was then, and its nature and performance in 1997. Hong Kong would provide the opportunity for the PLA to make a fresh start in the eyes of the world.

None of this was unknown, and even the slightest effort to consult recognised China analysts or their writings, which are widely available in the West, would have enabled the media to spread the word and to educate the public about this reforming army and its aim and immediate significance for Hong Kong, and indeed the world.

During this period before the handover there were, therefore, two sets of outsiders about to move in large numbers into Hong Kong. First, there were the PLA troops, whom we know had been hand-picked to carry out the important new tasks of defending Hong Kong as part of China and creating a new look for the Chinese army. These troops were young, proud and doubtless eager to shine after months of preparation, certainly apprehensive as to what might happen to them in the streets of Hong Kong (for they all knew the effect Tiananmen Square had had upon the world) shy perhaps, and not for a moment expecting to kill anyone; just hoping to get inside their barracks as quickly as possible. Secondly, there were the representatives of the media, hand-picked, the cream of their profession, each wanting to make his particular mark. The world's journalists eager to find their story, or to spot the hitch, the slip or the unexpected or the out-of-court that would please, not Army

Command, but the news editor or the director-general. However historic the occasion, diplomacy, speeches, marching back and forth and flags going up and down were still not enough to satisfy the market and secure a long enough concentration span. Spice of drama, subtext of tease and tension, was for these men and women the order of the day.

'the reputation of a powerful and civilised force.'

The PLA Hong Kong garrison is drawn from the 41st Division stationed on the Sino-Vietnamese border and the 42nd Division (1,500 troops) from Shenzhen, the army base for Guangdong Province. They were all chosen well in advance and specifically prepared for Hong Kong duty. The units may be from certain areas but the troops that comprise them come from all over China. And many of them are conscripts who are serving their compulsory 2–3 years with the forces. Deliberately many of them have very little Cantonese because the Commissars work on the principle of control through language – or lack of it. If you cannot chat to the locals you cannot really fraternise and this limits the possibilities of absorption into the Hong Kong lifestyle.

The Chinese do not, as yet, have a developed non-commissioned officer system which means officers often do jobs and basic training not done by officers in other armies. Now it is generally agreed that good NCOs are the backbone of any battalion, so this lack is proving a hindrance in the PLA's desire for modernisation. Many of the conscripts are peasants and unwilling soldiers and even amongst regulars there is high manpower wastage because, as pay is low, it is not the sought-after job the authorities would like it to be and turnover is high.

Educational standards, too, are lower than those required to provide the new technocrats for the streamlined army they plan. But all these matters are under review and the increasing professionalism amongst the officers below flag rank, who tend to be more concerned with such matters as keeping their vehicles on the road or having enough rice to feed their men, bodes well for the future. Indeed, not only is the average officer at or below the rank of colonel not political; he is not even *thinking* about doctrine.

The soldiers' tour of duty lasts from six months to one year on a rotational system. All leave, holidays and even weekends will be spent back across the border at base in Shenzhen. At present, pay is poor – in Hong Kong terms disastrous – at roughly the equivalent of £5 per month. There are rumours that it may be increased, though lack of money also helps to limit the possibility of fraternisation. So far the PLA has been very quiet and retiring, as they are extremely anxious to avoid any incidents that could be seized on to show them in a bad light but if it is decided they should have a higher profile they would obviously change their personnel and their rules.

It could be that, in time, Beijing will decide that fewer troops are needed in the city, as the Hong Kong Police have everything so well controlled and their tactical units are trained and experienced in minimum-force riot control. Not for nothing did Beijing come to Hong Kong for advice after Tiananmen Square. And the PLA's troops in

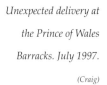

Unexpected delivery at the Prince of Wales Barracks. July 1997.

(Craig)

Shenzhen would be near enough for any external defence.

Further areas of PLA jurisdiction are customs, transport across the border in search and rescue, border security and smuggling control. If they want to keep a low profile in Hong Kong they have to keep strict control of the border on their side otherwise the Hong Kong Police could be overwhelmed.

Initially, of course, the presence of Chinese troops was an important and essential sign of sovereignty. Indeed, at the pre-midnight ceremony on 30 June, General Xiong Ziren, the political commissar of the Hong Kong garrison, said the formal take-over of the Prince of Wales Barracks symbolised the PLA's assumption of defence responsibilities; and in a speech read to the troops to be stationed in the Special Administrative Region (Hong Kong) at a farewell ceremony in Shenzhen, President Jiang Zemin declared 'the presence of Chinese troops is an important *sign* of sovereignty'. He added that the garrison must work for the long-term prosperity and stability of Hong Kong. 'I hope you will conduct yourselves and abide by the laws so as to establish for the Hong Kong garrison the reputation of a powerful and civilised force.'

Meanwhile, their presence, however low-key, is a clear signal to the rest of China that Hong Kong really is reunited with the Motherland. What do they do, these troops? At the moment, because of Tiananmen Square and its aftermath, there is more political education. There is concern at the top level at the hesitancy displayed by some units over their Beijing orders and the preoccupation with matters economic at the expense of matters Party. Hence the influence of the Political Commissar is currently strong.

It should be noted, in passing, that according to the Basic Law, business activity in Hong Kong is strictly limited. However, around three per cent of the property purchasing market in Hong Kong will, we understand, be PLA investment.

The troops are lightly armed, their biggest item being their armoured personnel carriers similar to those used by the Hong Kong Police, and will have little equipment to maintain. The garrison in Hong Kong will comprise an infantry brigade, an airforce helicopter group and a fleet of patrol boats and transport vessels. Hong Kong is above all, a political mission. The PLA troops are a Show Force – to let everyone know that Hong Kong is, once again, Chinese. As a local commentator said, 'What they're here to do is a lot of marching back and forth'. Whether and how this approach will change depends on the wider political influences and on how relaxed and confident Beijing and/or the Shenzhen generals become.

At the Commander British Forces' house, Hong Kong. Generals Liu and Dutton. 1997.

(JSPRS)

FULL, TOO,
OF THE UNQUIET SPIRITS

The Black Watch HQ, as already mentioned, on Stonecutters' Island is linked to Kowloon by a new highway running past busy shipyards. But as we found it more convenient to use the military launches to move between Stonecutters', Kowloon and Hong Kong Island, we tended to regard it as still cut off by sea. It is an area full of poignant history and intriguing possibilities and one to which, as matters stand, no outsider can now go.

In contrast to Prince of Wales Barracks, the buildings at Stonecutters' are low with not a lift in sight and spread out across a wide area. There are a number of rare examples of Victorian military architecture and artillery emplacements with underground magazines and vaulted tunnels which you can still see, though some are in considerable disrepair and others are overgrown ruins. Among the buildings are football pitches, lawns, tropical flowers, military detritus, birds, snakes, rats, spiders.

A Jock explained, amongst other things, that he didn't mind the snakes – they moved away from you – or the rats – because they were just going about their business – but that spiders were a different kettle of fish altogether. 'A spider comes intae ma room ... ah'm oot o'there!,' he said emphatically. The other day he'd moved some furniture and 'there was this bugger, big as a teacup. Ah'm tellin' ye, ah moved only two or three seconds slower than the speed o' light!', and he gave an

Major General Dutton, CBE, awards Long Service and Good Conduct medals. Stonecutters' Island 1997. (Frank Proctor)

BW Commanding Officer compares rehearsal notes with the Garrison Sergeant Major. Stonecutters' Island 1997.

(Craig)

involuntary shudder.

With the signing of the convention of Peking in 1860, part of the Kowloon Peninsula and Stonecutter's Island were ceded to Britain 'with a view to maintaining law and order in and about the Harbour of Hong Kong'. A prison was built in the mid-1860s but in 1890 an Ordinance was passed, making Stonecutter's Island a military area and a fortress was created in the western section of Victoria Harbour. In addition, the construction of five batteries was completed in 1899, but by the late 1930s all but the West Battery had fallen into disuse, due to changes in strategic planning. Stonecutter's became a naval island in 1905 and stayed under the control of the Royal Navy until 1957, when it reverted once more to the British Army. A huge armament depot was built between the wars, which included 11 large underground magazines. In the mid-1930s, the Admiralty also set up a very powerful intelligence intercept station on the island which was the most important of its kind in the Far East until the outbreak of the war with Japan in 1941.

There was much of interest. St Barbara's Chapel had been built as part of the gaol. The complex, finished in 1866, was never used as a prison, but was used to house patients during a massive outbreak of smallpox in 1871. By July 1873 it was in such a poor state of repair that a typhoon two years later destroyed everything except for the Gatehouse – used as the Black Watch HQ – two towers, the Prison Governor's House, now the Officers' Mess, and two lengths of stone wall.

After a series of fires, the Hong Kong Army Depot Police who guarded the ammunition depot, were manned solely by Sikhs – because their religion does not allow smoking. The transition from a European-officered force to an all-Sikh force took place in 1965–66. Disbanded in October 1994, this was the last Sikh unit to be associated with the British Army, ending a link with this magnificent warrior caste going back over 200 years. The Japanese ran a snake farm on the island to produce snake-bite serum for their forces fighting in Asia. At the end of the war they released the snakes, which is why the island has some non-indigenous species. Luckily, most of them do not like the heat that rises from the many concrete roads and paths and they have never been a problem for the inhabitants. The Quartermaster told me that while he had been escorting a group of government officials over the island, one of them asked if they often saw snakes. 'Right on cue,' said the QM, 'a big one, the biggest I've ever seen, a real whopper, crossed the path in front of them.' 'What's that?' queried the pale official. 'Och, that's nothing …

just a wee one,' replied the QM and chuckled quietly to himself for the rest of the day.

He also said that some macaws had been released from the Zoological Park in 1941 when the bombing started, and pointed out those that are still left. Some 300 black-eared kites live all the year round on the island and the Eurasian hoopoe bred successfully there for the first time in 1993.

Stonecutters' Island is full, too, of the unquiet spirits of those tortured under unbelievably cruel conditions by Japanese occupation forces. The Mess had been their HQ and, with its pleasant beaches and tranquil environment, Stonecutter's had served as a rest and recreation centre for Japanese officers. They built a Geisha House on a hill – still known as Geisha Hill – where they used to bring Chinese women and abuse and torture them. After the war, it was immediately razed to the ground. The Chinese will not go near the site even now, and some say if you walk up the hill of an evening, you can still hear faint screams wafted on the breeze. The QM's normally genial expression vanished as he told this story and I thought of my uncle, who had survived the brutalities of a Japanese prison camp only to die of cancer a few years after his return home; and of his deep loathing for the sons of bushido.

Stonecutters' also houses the Medical Officer and his staff, a vital element of any battalion. The doctor loved the job and Hong Kong. But, of course, the heat had to be watched; when the temperature went over 32°C, a flag would be hoisted to warn everyone to stop doing anything energetic. Two soldiers had died previously, but not in Hong Kong, and one had had a heart attack. He was hoping no one would be seriously ill over the 30 June period, as he was not allowed to leave *anybody* behind. Otherwise normal ailments, plus removal of the odd tattoo – an old girlfriend's name perhaps – kept him busy. He had to deal with a certain amount of absence-related stress amongst families. Army life is hard on marriage. He himself was returning to a six-week-old baby.

The medical sergeant who gave us our second hepatitis B injections had a butterfly touch. He said they *always* changed the needle after *each* injection; it was possible to use them more than once if they were

Catering for all circumstances – A break during rehearsals, Stonecutters' Island 1997 . (Craig)

thoroughly sterilised but one jab blunts a needle; muscle is thick and resistant. We both felt nothing at all. When he leaves the army he plans to take up a civilian career as a practice manager in the National Health Service – a good example of army life being a career in itself but leading on to further employment. This is essential if the army is to find the quality recruits it needs.

We went back to the parade ground with its splendid views over once sandy beaches towards Kowloon, where many handover rehearsals were held under a sizzling sun – soldiers, bands and Pipes and Drums, sometimes all together and sometimes separately in different areas. We later came to the Officers' Mess for the last Black Watch party and Beating Retreat on 6 June. With the pipes and drums, this particular ceremony always has its emotional aspects and this twilight summer evening, with its special significance, was no exception. It was the regiment's last chance to say goodbye and thanks to Hong Kong friends and acquaintances because, next day, most of the Mess furniture would be packed up for shipment to the UK.

We all stood on the side steps leading from the terrace to where the pipes and drums were performing on a small area of grass. This somewhat restricted free movement but only served to underline their

New, deep-water harbour built for PLA Navy, Stonecutters' Island 1997. (Craig)

expertise. As nostalgic tones filled the air, I watched the different faces beside me and wondered if this was the last time the pipes would be heard on Stonecutters' Island. And then it was over and it was back into the cool of the Mess, a buffet supper, chat and dancing.

The Ceilidh Band was an extremely lively trio – fiddle, keyboard and drums – well wired up and producing a truly reverberating beat. Alas, the layout of the Mess was not ideal for reels and strathspeys but the Black Watch, ever adaptable, used all available space to great effect. The QM mingled benignly with the guests. He wore the contented smile of a man who had just finished 'handing over' Stonecutters' Island (or at least the required documents) to the Hong Kong government. He sipped his beer with satisfaction.

I watched a retired Black Watch colonel dancing with his wife in the same eightsome as the current commanding officer. Earlier I had noticed this man in profile, as he stood near the top of the Mess steps during Beating Retreat. As the Drum Major marched forward to salute at the finish, he had drawn himself up – face like a hawk – and, whether through a trick of the light or my own heightened emotions, the years fell away and I thought he was actually going to take the salute. But the moment passed.

There were two scheduled launches back to Kowloon and Central, otherwise you were on your own. We had opted, with a busy day following, for the early boat; but when I glanced at my watch it had already gone.

CHAPTER 13

THE MAIN CASUALTY IS TRUTH

The successful wildlife watcher keeps entirely still and avoids making any noise or recognisable difference in occupation of space; the additional presence of an observer at the experiment of a quantum physicist will inevitably alter the way things go, destabilise what has happened, ultimately making the outcome different.

The injection into Hong Kong, just before the handover, of 6,000 media men and women and their equipment from press and broadcasting

A TV director states his requirements. Stonecutters' Island 1997.

(Frank Proctor)

organisations all over the world transformed the atmosphere of the place (and our own presence there) not out of all recognition, for much went on the same, but by the introduction of a sense of loss, a notion that a previous collective composure, a grace and ordering amongst the Hong Kong people in their movement towards political change, had been violated.

In contrast to the slight, self-contained Chinese who quietly negotiated their passage along crowded streets, seeming to anticipate movement around them and respecting the space of others rather than invading it, the media men and women, the Europeans and Americans especially, with cameras swirling about their persons, conveyed a sort of insistence, or at least an expectation, that a path be opened up before them. Thus, Hong Kong felt invaded.

Was it necessary to bring 6,000 media people to Hong Kong, and would not reasonable human co-operation combined with modern technology have catered for world coverage well enough? One man said seriously that there were more BBC people in Hong Kong than soldiers in the garrison – not true, if only because of the influx of military bands flown in three weeks before the handover, but the quip was a good one and did the rounds.

A BW sergeant does his show for the British Forces' Broadcasting Service, Hong Kong.

(Frank Proctor)

The formal events marking the change of sovereignty were to take place along a short stretch of harbour, itself not far from Government House, and all within a distance roughly the same as along the banks of the Thames between Westminster and Waterloo Bridges. This concentration of activity and attention into such a small area constituted in itself an extraordinary handover phenomenon. And although some journalists and reporters arrived early enough to savour Hong Kong's final days under British rule and stayed on to compare them with its early days as part of China, most television crews came with just enough time to set up equipment, run through rehearsals and transmit, live, on the day. The full, massive presence of the media was thus concentrated not only into a small area but also into a relatively brief spell of time, and the intensity of the general atmosphere thus became even more charged.

While the presence and activity of the media men vulgarised the mood and face of Hong Kong, some individual directors attempted to alter, sometimes successfully, an event or scene that they were assigned to record or transmit. A BBC television crew requested that the lights of *Britannia* and HMS *Chatham* be lit earlier than the strictly observed naval time to facilitate an evening shoot: and a Scottish television crew asked the Black Watch to perform a special programme for the sole benefit of their cameras. Though hard-pressed with other demands and duties, the Black Watch agreed, rehearsed and otherwise prepared a suitable programme, only to be told by telephone when the time came that the idea lacked enough 'appeal' and that the crew would not be filming. Such an example touches upon the innate tensions between the needs of broadcast production and the discipline of the function or performance they record or film, whether ceremonial, parliamentary, sporting, military. Such tensions form a subtext of more or less continuous dialogue and intermittent conflict about the extent to which activity or ritual may acceptably be adjusted, rigged or altered to satisfy the demands of network scheduling or the niceties of artistic touch.

Such problems are a constant test of training and character and, in Hong Kong, in a political climate of bickering at the highest level, with its consequent trickle-down impact, and under a hot sun, with record humidity, were well fielded as symptoms of over-heating of one kind or another and regarded with a fit sense of the ridiculous. But, in fact, those occasions, minor in themselves, were symptoms of a more serious malaise and the Hong Kong experience, in mid-1997, provided demonstrations of the media functioning at peaks of excellence and at depths of bad manners and taste.

In the early days of BBC cuts, veteran foreign correspondents spoke of their deep concerns at the logical progression of a consultancy-led 'vision': fewer correspondents, more ground to cover – literally as well as metaphorically – for those who remained, less time for interpretation or analysis of events. In the round an inevitable threat to quality of output. All this was compounded by intense and growing pressures by BBC bosses for 'live' input into news and current affairs programmes, the foreign correspondent being hustled to provide constant hot 'up-dates' from 'on the spot' as well as detail of local response to events and political comment. It was increasingly difficult, they said, to find time to complete a considered assessment of one situation before being dispatched to the next.

Today in both television and radio broadcasting, we have ever-increasing doses of 'vox pop' and 'what did you see and how do you feel?' The morning news covers not just what happened overnight but what some minister will announce that afternoon, the substance of his speech, how we shall all be affected and so on. In fact, 'news' has become not only about what has just passed but what is about to be so that we live our lives more and more ahead of ourselves. The threat to the quality of broadcast news inherent in this obsession with immediacy does not alter the fact that, along with the moving image itself, it is the essence and the distinctive imperative of television. Hence, for this young medium, as in Greek tragedy, in its very nature lie the seeds of its own destruction.

Radio is not tied to the immediate to the same degree as television and has the advantage when it comes to looking ahead, for words may carry the imagination a long way forward whilst it is impossible to film the future, however close. The context of newspaper and magazine

Sir Les Patterson (Dame Edna to some) brings culture to the wild Highlanders. 1997.

(Frank Proctor)

output, though as up to date as technology will allow, is essentially retrospective, reflective and cannot compete at all in the field of the immediate. But the medium of speculation is the word and the newspaper may look to the future and consider, too, what it may bring. And sometimes the newspaper (though not the magazine) will positively revel in the imminent.

One example from the past. At the start of the Gulf War, in 1990, CNN showed vivid pictures of missiles – 'smart-bombs' – being remotely directed through windows, round corners etc, in an impressive display of controlled aggression which made a great impact on other viewing countries including China, which was shocked at how far behind it was in the new technologies of war. CNN's presented picture was, in fact, untrue. Only about three in ten missiles ever worked as shown. There were often mishits, duds and malfunctions and the impression given was a gross distortion. The network had set its own agenda and shown not what was actually happening but, through edit and exaggeration, a more dramatic version of what was going on. A deliberate distortion of the facts played its key part in the battle for audience ratings and, not for the first time, nor for the last, the main casualty was truth.

CHAPTER 14

THE BUSINESS IS BUSINESS

It was always hot and usually wet in Hong Kong over the handover period, but if the weather was not worth mentioning conversationally, the ups and downs of the Hang Seng index were in a different league and all the handover hype in the world could not make a dent in incessant talk of red chips and blue chips, rates of exchange and reserves. And if the Stock Market was not the place to generate some extra income – then it was the lottery, the racecourse, Macau Casino or the post-office counter selling the latest issue of stamps.

'The business is business,' they say in Hong Kong, and we were told, hardly less often, by a Hong Kong television advertisement, 'What can be imagined can be achieved'.

How has Hong Kong achieved the almost unimaginable? Clues abound. Moving about the streets we daily saw workmen, in great heat and humidity, digging roads, constructing huge areas of scaffolding, bamboo pole by bamboo pole, cleaning windows without the aid of machinery, at 40th and 50th floor level, and, at night, hosing sides of buildings and surfaces of motorways; feats of slog and sweat, of relentless bending and stretching of back and arm, all without apparent fear of hard work, or height. All these are direct descendants, in spirit at least, of those early stone-cutters in Hong Kong who wielded tools or built by hand the first stone walls, quays and dwellings; and of carriers of bamboo poles and wicker baskets; of labourers who, small load by small load, tipped fill from their junks and sampans to create land where sea had been; of men and women, who, in the mid-20th Century, crossing the border from China to escape violence and turmoil, further transformed the territory. These were Chinese, their contribution too often unacknowledged, or even forgotten, yet each a founder, literally, of modern Hong Kong.

When the English first settled in Hong Kong in the 1840s, after a naval party had raised the flag at Possession Point in 1841, it was neither barren nor uninhabited; nor was its granite the real attraction of 'the rock', but the deep waters of its adjacent harbour. For it was neither oil strike nor gold dig, diamond mine nor coal-face, that was to bring great wealth to Hong Kong but its port, originally from which to trade with the Chinese mainland. Then, after 1949 and the emergence of Communist rule in China, and later in the wake of trade embargoes following the war in Korea, Hong Kong turned to the business of

Seats of power. Left to right: Old Bank of China; Mandarin Oriental Hotel; Jardine Tower; Legco Building; and New Bank of China. (Craig)

126

China Club, Dining Room. (Craig)

exporting its own manufactured goods. Today, the Hong Kong economy is concentrated in service industries – shipping, banking, insurance, investment, involving increasingly massive input from the Chinese mainland. The port remains vital, now the biggest container port in the world and, from 1998, boasting the world's biggest airport sited on Lantau Island at Chek Lap Kok, accompanied by a further huge port development scheme.

Hong Kong's economic achievement, past and present, is beyond dispute but its future is the subject of much debate and anxiety. There are two main, widely diverging, prognoses for Hong Kong's economy. The most comforting line is that China itself wants Hong Kong to succeed and here lies Hong Kong's best insurance: if things were to go wrong in Hong Kong it would be bad news for China too; its own prestige would be damaged; foreign investors would divert capital; the growth of China's economy would slow down and this, in turn, would lead to social turmoil. Hong Kong is China's new trade showpiece, this argument goes, and China will make sure Hong Kong looks good.

The bleaker view is that in mainland China today business arrangements are 'looser' than in highly regulated Hong Kong and, furthermore, political consideration filtered down through Party officials may easily block or circumvent an inconvenient contract. Ways of maintaining social order in China are also corrupt and for this reason its government is unlikely, in the near future, to go in for modernisation; for some time to come it is likely that the Party will remain more influential, decisive and superior to all laws. Put another way, if China now were to adopt Hong Kong trade practice and regulation, rooted in the rule of law, and were to become, in its own trading, more open and professional, then the Communist Party would have to retreat. This is unlikely in the foreseeable future. Should Hong Kong become more influenced by China than China by Hong Kong, it is likely that within five years of the handover, Hong Kong may become just another Chinese city – an unreliable place for Westerners to do business.

This boils down to an issue of confidence – something which may take decades to build up, but no time at all to rock. Foreign investment – the continuation of international trust in Hong Kong – is the vital factor, which in turn means that Hong Kong's economic wellbeing is susceptible to some extent to events outside its own influence; for example, changes in the climate of international opinion towards China itself, as well, of course, as to its own rates of economic performance. There is a reliable barometer to watch, we were told: 'Watch the Shanghainese businessmen – if they go, then you'll know it's all over'.

The crucial contribution of the press, too, in maintaining stability in international confidence in Hong Kong cropped up again and again. One travel agent claimed that in July and August 1997 there had been a big drop in visitors especially from the UK and Europe; perhaps some had come earlier in the year (presumably to avoid the handover, including inflated hotel prices), but the 80 per cent drop she blamed mainly on 'negative' reporting, especially in the UK. Travel agents from the UK had been flown over free of charge to encourage them to promote Hong Kong as a good place to stay.

Two colourful criticisms of newspaper reporting centred on the same club, with some irony. The first: 'All foreign correspondents are basically alcoholics, and British Ex-pats always moan ... so, in Hong Kong, the correspondents go to the Foreign Correspondents' Club and get drunk and talk to the moaning Ex-pats and then go off and write about Hong Kong being down the tube'. The second (made over drinks in the Foreign Correspondents' Club itself:): 'Foreign correspondents are ex-Vietnam, ex-Korea, and suffer from consequent mind-set – China is bad, QED'. A successful young small-businessman put it succinctly: 'We could do without the negative reporting.'

Ted Thomas, who has lived in Hong Kong for over 40 years and is a well-known Hong Kong freelance journalist and broadcaster, has devoted much time recently to mounting a challenge to the generally negative reporting about Hong Kong to the rest of the world and to encouraging better informed writing.

Fear of the spread of corruption from China into the Special Administrative Region and a bad press for Hong Kong abroad were two main threats to the continuing confidence of the foreign investor. Would Hong Kong adopt Chinese mainland ways or would it be the other way round? And what about the new Chief Executive, Mr Tung Chee Hwa? He was not in any sense chosen by, or even as a result of consultation with, the Hong Kong people themselves.

'I like him,' our reporter friend from the Hong Kong *Sunday Standard* said, 'but the screws are tightening.' She herself was to leave Hong Kong soon after the handover to further her career in Australia. Tung had made a good beginning, talking amicably to people in the streets, in a way some had forecast he would never do and pledging an ambitious programme for the new administration, including a massive home-building programme.

There was much optimism in Hong Kong and one of the more positive outcomes of the change of sovereignty was described eloquently, as a new sense of identity and of belonging for the Hong Kong Chinese, who make up 97 per cent of the population. Now that British rule was over and Hong Kong was China once more, there would be a renewed enthusiasm, a protectiveness allied to possession, which might bring new habits of thinking and planning in the longer term. For previously, there had been a mood of transience, a feeling that Hong Kong was a sort of transit camp to which people came to make their pile and then move on. This rootlessness had, in turn, engendered a culture of short-term values. One vivid conversationalist, who believes that the ancient English cathedral and English church choral music are two of the world's most amazing phenomena, said that in Hong Kong any building over ten years of age was considered too old, and promptly bulldozed.

The state of Hong Kong's environment and the serious threat to what survives of its wild places (still a significant amount, including its country parks and its lovely shoreline) is one area that would benefit from a longer perspective. Urgent, too, is the need to improve the quality of air and water in the Region.

Edward Stokes, photographer and environmentalist living and working in Hong Kong, has identified key forces behind modern environmental degradation, not least, in the case of Hong Kong, continuing public complacency. He has warned that two issues, conservation education and the post-1997 administration's attitude to controls over development, should be key considerations if the new Region's story is to be one of continuing success. A further threat, he believes, which may well gain strength from reunification, comes from the Guangdong area of China, which borders the northern part of the New Territories. This province he sees as a potential source of both pollution and hasty, ill-conceived schemes which may have a disastrous impact upon the Hong Kong environment.

As to business in Hong Kong, we found in post-handover days an overriding optimism, most cynically expressed along the lines that in pursuit of profit Hong Kongers can be counted upon to adapt to *any* new *modus vivendi*.

Historically, Hong Kong has stood up well to challenge and change. Investment in the territory was always regarded as high risk but the risk was compensated for by the fruits of high profit made possible by the huge pool of cheap labour, substantially supplied by the steady influx of émigrés from mainland China. When, in time, increasing cost of both labour and industrial rents became a serious threat to successful business, a solution was found: factories were moved north across the border and into the mainland where costs were relatively cheap. Today, Hong Kong business interests spread rapidly across China in all directions.

Hong Kong also has a well developed infrastructure, not typical of Asia. Travelling from point to point in Hong Kong was always a pleasure during our stay except when there were serious traffic delays on the main route from Taipo to the new container port, due to extensive road reconstruction involving a complicated network of overpass and bridge. This led to congestion, even blockage, in the evening rush. But on these slow journeys we were able to witness the rapidity of work and change in appearance that are distinguishing features of life in Hong Kong. During our stay, too, we watched the transformation of the newly-reclaimed area in front of the Prince of Wales Building, which was made ready just in time – deliberately – for royal and military ceremony over the handover period.

While there is much ground for optimism in Hong Kong's economic future, there is, along with the issues of international confidence and investment, a further question: 'Is Hong Kong's success a bubble?' Land is at the root of everything in Hong Kong. This, of course, is true in other parts of the world. In the United States, for example, the westward frontier movement over vast tracts of virgin land refined a resourcefulness and an ability to stand upon one's own feet that is a remarkable match to the spirit of today's Hong Kong people. But in Hong Kong it is the small amount of land that dictates its massive value. Attempting, in October 1996, to set a specific value upon the Prince of Wales Building which was the HQ of British Forces in Hong Kong and located in Central, the Defence Land Agent advised that as there had been no sales in the area for over a year, there were no available comparisons and suggested it might be best to use as a base land values of the previous year which had been 'in the order of a million Hong Kong dollars per square metre'. It is this scarcity and high cost of land and the consequent high price of property which, according to one financial expert, will be the death-knell of Hong Kong within five years of the handover. He believes, too, that the much-vaunted 'free' economy of Hong Kong is a myth, a nonsense, and that, on the contrary, Hong Kong's is a 'contrived' economy. All non-privately-owned land in Hong

Kong (except St John's Anglican Cathedral) belongs to the Hong Kong government, whose practice has been to manipulate the amount of land released for selling at levels significantly below market demand, thus keeping prices, and government income, high. (An undesirable off-shoot of this practice was profitable scope for speculators, a problem the new Chief Executive declared the new administration would vigorously tackle.) The fact that no government bonds were issued in Hong Kong arose from the simple fact that the government not only had no debts but billions of dollars in reserve. The challenge to the new administration would be to provide, in these difficult circumstances, enough housing for the fast-growing population.

A businessman told us that he believed that the great secret of Hong Kong's success stemmed from its flourishing middle-class, a phenomenon crucially lacking in South Africa, where he had formerly worked. He considers that danger for Hong Kong lies in the continuing exodus of middle-class men and women who, having worked their way up both career and social ladders, are now seeking jobs in countries like Singapore, where suitable housing is more cheaply available.

A further point made was that numbers of professional people manage to avoid this obstacle through benefit of government housing which they can rent at cheap rates. Into this category fall thousands of teachers and police, for example, whose rent may amount to about one eighth of what they would have to pay for equivalent housing in the open market. As many of these beneficiaries were British under the old administration, their privileged circumstances were often the root of hostility between local Chinese and the Ex-pat community.

Property has always been a key issue in Hong Kong, although in the mid-20th Century it was the housing of the poor which received major attention. While the moral imperative spurred the massive rehousing programme, which accommodated the poor in cheap-rent government tower blocks, there were underlying benefits also for business interests. The provision of cheap shelter enabled employers to keep wages low. Governor Maclehose's vision for the 1970s, which he announced in 1971, was a ten-year plan to rehouse 1,800,000 people, through a strategy of 'vertical development' – huge tower blocks built within a number of 'resettlement estates', which are still a striking and increasing feature of Hong Kong today.

There seemed a parallel mood change in the UK and in Hong Kong in mid-1997. We left Britain in May, two days after the General Election and, a month after our return, the death of Diana, Princess of Wales evoked strong expressions of public feeling which, in some way, seemed a rejection of past priorities of self-interest and seemed to point towards a more responsible social outlook. In Hong Kong, too, there were signs of disenchantment with the high priority given to material values. These were no longer enough, and notions of community and welfare-provision were becoming more important in the Hong Kong agenda. In both Britain and Hong Kong one sensed the maturing of desires to reach beyond the measurable.

Housing the Government plans to replace. (Craig)

CHAPTER 15

WELL, WE HAVE AN UMBRELLA

Hong Kong has a big share of social problems – ironically, in part, because of its wealth but in part, too, because of its geographical position; just across the water from Vietnam, just across the border from mainland China, close to Thailand and, relatively, to Nepal. So many people want to go and be there. Often they come, not seeking the positive – freedom of expression and the rule of law – but rather, in flight from some nightmare of persecution, torture or destitution, or from a life in some other way fragile or ill-dealt.

Watch towers on border.
Note fencing on both
sides of path. (Craig)

So the desire to come to Hong Kong lies not only in the hearts of the go-getting and rich, the skilled and clever, but also amongst those deprived of money, skill or education. And these are not necessarily unwelcome, for they are often tough, adaptable, durable, and for decades have provided vast pools of cheap labour, the foundation of Hong Kong's prosperity.

Hong Kong is half filled with émigrés or children of émigrés, who fled in pursuit not of the high-life and of glamour but for betterment, which meant improvement but still a life of grind and toil. In their flight they showed themselves to be spirited, robust, the latest wave of those, who, for centuries, have qualified as refugees from persecution, hunger and hopelessness. Nor do such roots necessarily lead to manifestations of self-pity or resentment, nor to high levels of expectation or demand.

A young reporter friend insists that poverty – not starvation or destitution, but poverty – is a state of mind. It is relative. She told of a couple who had fled from their troubles in China and set up on a pier in Hong Kong, based under the shade of their umbrella. They do not consider they are badly off: 'Well, we have an umbrella,' they say.

Window cleaner,

Central district. (Craig)

Less reconciled to their lot, it seems, are those refugees from Vietnam who are still in Hong Kong camps. Hampered by criminal records, drug usage, age or illness, they are proving to be the refugees most difficult to place elsewhere. They find it hard to acknowledge the very limited framework of options open to them. One United Nations worker in a camp described their spirit as 'obdurate', not as a criticism, but in recognition of their indomitable will. Her role, she said, is to offer them compassion mixed with realism.

For most of us it is scarcely possible to imagine that savage cocktail, a mixture of fear and hope which drives illegal immigrants

Inspecting a fishing boat for drugs or illegal immigrants. 1997.

(JSPRS)

towards the high wire fencing bordering mainland China and Hong Kong, and to risk empalement upon its barbed top, or quick capture and the uncertain consequences of an enforced return to China. Some remain so desperate they will try again and again. Terrible, too, to contemplate, the desperation of men and women who jump from the tops of tower blocks, their best or only option, leaving behind their shoes, neatly laid, signifying their intention to commit suicide. 'FFH' a police inspector responsible will write; 'Fell From Height'.

As she looked north from the balcony of our flat towards the hills of Kowloon which lay in evening darkness, a young woman police officer spoke to us about Hong Kong's missing children. 'How can Hong Kong be a happy place when so many run away from home?' she asked. Police scour streets daily and some children are spotted, some even retrieved. Those who remain unfound may have had in mind – may even arrive at – a particular destination, often attracted by promise abroad. These include girls who set off to become waitresses in another country but who on arrival discover things are not as they had expected.

For these and for thousands of others living in Hong Kong, the business is not business at all but a clinging-on, a bleak survival. Many manage to keep going above the level of destitution but during the handover period new difficulties were emerging which compound existing problems and create new complexities. If the transition itself had appeared smooth on the surface, to some of these people the change was immediate, dramatic, even traumatic.

'Do you speak with tongues?'

'We're their last resort. That's when they come to us, when everything else has failed. Do you speak with tongues?' asked our guide, and we soon witnessed for ourselves her own fluent Cantonese which, along with her Christian conviction, engendered a warm rapport with the drug addicts she was taking us to meet. As she guided us along the early evening streets, she told us about the work of the Society of St Stephen's, and, when we reached the large and dilapidated room where meetings were held, a few men and women were already there. Some were talking amongst themselves, others sitting alone, though seeming quite at home – gathered somehow. After six o'clock more and more came until, by seven-thirty, the room was brimful.

One old man was there to be with his son, who himself was sitting on the other side of the room and who had been addicted to drugs for years. 'We've tried everything,' the old man said. Many spoke some English, a few, a lot. Some had been hooked for years, others much less. Like a caught fish, if you struggled hard enough early on, you might get away, but the point would come when only a miraculous act could loosen the grip. 'Come and talk, then we'll pray together.'
People who themselves had suffered earlier addiction but whose situation had improved, or people who considered themselves cured, were there, voluntarily, to be with those who had come there dependent, or desperate. The hours were spent mainly in groups of two or three, each client the subject of the complete attention of one or two helpers. Later came hand-holding or arm-arounding, then, eyes closed, minutes of quietly spoken prayer and occasional shared silence.

In her book *Chasing the Dragon*, Jackie Pullinger described her years of work tackling the problems of drug addiction and the ruined lives of those who fall into it and of those close to them. And when, later in the evening, she arrived to talk to the then encircled gathering, there was no doubt about the intensity of attention given to her message – spoken in fluent Cantonese which we didn't understand, though we were told it was the story in which Lazarus is raised from the dead by Jesus.

What was clear, however, was the pleasure derived from the hymn-singing that followed her words and the transparent joy in the full-throated alleluias, the climax of each verse. In Hong Kong thousands of men and women lead the most fragmented and wretched drug-addicted existence. But whatever the rate of cure derived from these particular meetings, there is, for those who give them a try, a sureness of welcome that is genuine, a few hours' break from despair and momentary kindlings of self-esteem.

'Fear and misery … lurk in the shadows.'

The policy of distinction between 'refugee' and 'migrant' arose out of problems stemming from the arrival into Hong Kong in 1989 of 33,000 Vietnamese 'boat people', which created an urgent need to draw some line between those of greater and lesser need to stay away from their homeland. During 1990, the line having thus been drawn, many who had returned to Vietnam had reported that the days of automatic settlement were over. This discouragement was reflected in a drop in numbers arriving from Vietnam; by November that year, there had been only 5,000 newcomers.

Those deemed 'migrants' were allocated to special detention camps in Hong Kong to which they were confined absolutely; no working in Hong Kong, nor expeditions but simply a holding point until in time they were returned to Vietnam. We walked up to the site above High Reservoir Detention Camp, near Sai Kung, on our first Sunday in Hong Kong, from which came the sound of loud, canned pop music, interrupted by barked announcements. The place was almost surrounded by water but there was no sailing for inmates, despite the boats moored nearby. When we left, in early August, the camp had been

Pillar Point refugee camp. (Craig)

closed down. One good point about these depressing places was the absence of drug-trafficking – not a claim which now even Pillar Point, the Vietnamese camp, could make, though the trafficking there was significantly less than three or four years previously, thanks partly to assiduous police work and partly to the vigilance of Jardine Gurkha security guards. 'There are no needles now,' we were told firmly. Earlier, Chinese triads had seen a quick way to make money by operating there.

There seemed to be some tension between police, who had worked in the refugee camps and some camp workers themselves. The police had little regard for the organisational skills of the UN administrators and workers and were impatient with what they deemed manifestations of 'over-protectiveness' of some workers to the extent, it was claimed, that sometimes it had become impossible to deal properly with the criminal elements. Camp workers were unduly obstructive when the police tried to take positive action or to arrest. They are always using this word 'protection', the police said.

Preeta Law, UNHCR Durable Solutions Officer, commented that protection was their brief, but she did add that there was some truth in past police criticism. The camp workers, on the other hand, claimed that sometimes refugees were in sore need of protection because on occasion the weak were 'set up' and the real culprit was not always the refugee the police had questioned. But police, too, firmly insisted that they had much sympathy for most of the refugees who were decent people, understandably seeking to better their lives. 'About 80 per cent are nice people,' one ex-Chief Inspector said, 'but 20 per cent are nasties, so selfish they would do almost anything – even kill their own.' The *South China Morning Post*, especially, but other newspapers too, had accused the police of beating refugees. 'Untrue' was the comment here, but in 'Correctives' people *had* been beaten. And the papers never reported the good things the police did, such as holding special parties for refugee children.

Yet another viewpoint was that of an ex-manager of a camp who said that tough eggs amongst the refugees meant good police back-up of camp staff was essential. But the support was not there, he said, the police were simply not interested. An adapted container was available as a retreat during a riot but you could only survive there for about seven minutes and would need help quickly. The Gurkha guards however, had been 'unfailingly wonderful'. To keep the record straight, the ex-Chief Inspector and the ex-camp manager quoted here had known each other and in the past had worked in the same camp; each spoke well of the other.

The current camp manager at Pillar Point, himself a former Gurkha soldier, said that in a refugee camp he had previously managed and which was by then closed down, the mere threat of removal to another camp had been enough to change behaviour of troublesome residents. Circumstances there had been more favourable because the camp was sited on an island and the atmosphere thus one of relative calm.

In the past, the press, too, had provided problems for those in charge of the camps. The British administration had been reluctant to allow them access to the camps, fearing (justifiably) that refugees might take the opportunity of their presence to highlight their concerns. At times of riot and hunger strike, press helicopters had sometimes added to the disturbance and press reports had distorted events, emphasising the drama of the occasion. But this press exclusion, it was eventually considered, had resulted in an abundance of myths and rumours and shortly before the handover it had been decided to try a new strategy and to encourage reporters to interview refugees who had volunteered for repatriation, perhaps even to accompany some back to Vietnam and to follow through their story there. Some had done so. A few days after our visit we noticed a front page Hong Kong press photograph of a roof-top protest at Pillar Point.

Questions remained after the handover. At the time of our visit, on 21 July, there had been no new policy change. 'We are waiting to see what the new Provisional Government will do.' Many refugees had left before the handover, 'but what will happen to those who remain ... the dregs?'

And what of those who look after the refugees? One British worker was contemplating the approaching to school-age of his own children and the possibility of the camp one day closing down for one reason or another. He loved living on the island of Cheung Chau, especially, he said, as the family enjoyed its beautiful, quiet beaches. Should he return to England? Did he really want to leave all this? The Jardine Gurkha Guards, too, were wondering about their future in this new part of China. Their own reputation as guards in the camps was very high and in those camps where they had had full responsibility for security everything had been tightly and equably run.

Fear of change seemed to preoccupy some of the better off and some of the worst off, but perhaps amongst the poor it was the improbability of difference in their lives, a future of sameness, endlessly, that filled their minds with apprehension. The most vulnerable are often unable to articulate their troubles and at times would not be referred to at all were it not for the voices of people like Martin Lee and another well-known member of the pre-July Legislative Council, Emily Lau, who openly warned that deprivation and suffering would weigh most heavily on the poor, that they would be hardest hit if basic freedoms were sacrificed in the interests of prosperity. Suffering silently could become a long and lonely business for those at the edge of society if it were not for the moral courage of such men and women. Someone told us that when Martin Lee was asked what Beijing might do to him if he continued saying such things he had replied, 'What does it matter?' Our informant concluded, 'to him there is truth, that is all'.

'Did you see any changes?' people repeatedly asked after we had returned to the UK. Changes in street or statistic are easily discerned and described, but fear and misery, fresh havoc in heart and mind, lurk in the shadows and remain out of print.

'No other country wants them.'

On one of the hottest, most humid days of our stay we arrived at the Vietnamese refugee camp at Pillar Point. A group of unprepossessing dwellings, built to serve for a short time as a transit camp for what were described to us as 'wretched souls', who had come out of one political situation into another, and were now causing a third. Some had been there for years, longer than they or the builders of the camp had anticipated. Immaculate, courteous but wholly observant guards, members of the Jardine Gurkha Security organisation, carefully noted our passport details and issued visitor's badges. We were taken through the high fence encircling the camp, and, passing a cluster of men and women who were later described as 'difficult', we moved into a quiet area across which moved a child clutching the hand of a smiling, slow walking guard who was, for the time being, entirely intent upon the concerns of his small companion. We, too, were being shepherded but by a member of the camp staff. The fence, he explained, was not to imprison the inhabitants but to keep out assorted unwanted visitors – drug-traffickers for example, the merely curious or press reporters and photographers, anyone who might disrupt attempts to keep an even tenor in the life of the camp.

Many of the inmates had left the site for a day's work in Hong Kong and the unemployed, too, were free to come and go as they pleased. The school was not open, so that the largest group of inmates we were to see was a cluster of very young children who lay on the floor in darkened silence, asleep or merely still, taking a siesta under the eyes of two young women who were pleasantly polite but did not encourage us to linger or to photograph.

Fathers of some of those children were away at work, possibly at the new airport being constructed at Chek Lap Kok, hoping to accumulate money to pay the family's way once they had left the camp and were resettled elsewhere. Some of the refugees had already left and were now successfully at work in Hong Kong, living in rented accommodation, saving money for a better future in Hong Kong or elsewhere; some were already living abroad in countries such as Britain, France, Canada and the US which had welcomed with enthusiasm their academic qualifications, skills and compassion.

Refugee. (Craig)

Other children had only their mothers with them in the camp, perhaps because their father was in prison, possibly had been there for a long period, or, in some cases, had been in and out of prison repeatedly. Some were children of divorced parents, or had found themselves amidst scenes of domestic violence. Amongst these relatively fit people there was a high level of frustration. The children could not be educated in Hong Kong schools, but only in Pillar Point's own school. The standard of education there was not low, and though the children we saw looked happy, their future was at best a question mark, for they were already socially and physically set apart from their young Hong Kong-born contemporaries. What was their future? Some of the families had greater problems having no recognised nationality, not Vietnamese, not Chinese, and living in a sort of limbo.

Those who remain in Pillar Point, about 1,300 altogether and the most difficult to settle, were being encouraged to return to Vietnam. Some had already gone back 'voluntarily', though not in all cases without some inducement. At an earlier stage, money had been offered to encourage repatriation, to pave the way in some sense to a new life, but this had to be stopped when it was realised that some enterprising Vietnamese were coming to Hong Kong, ostensibly as refugees but specifically in order to gain money by 'voluntarily' returning home! Now, though, if they refuse to go back to Vietnam, they must face the reality of doing what they can to make a living in Hong Kong. It is here that some find difficulty in coming to terms with reality, sometimes the hard fact that no other country wants them. At this point obduracy does *not* overcome.

'Some hands are washed.'

Quite by coincidence, a prearranged visit to a meeting of the new Provisional Legislature in Central was the occasion of a tabled discussion about aspects of the refugee problem. All visitors were provided with headphones, giving a running translation in English or Cantonese, the business being conducted in both languages. A lengthy agenda gave details of questions to be asked, by whom, and which official would formally answer, before discussion from the floor.

At this meeting of the Provisional Legislature, we were interested to watch its President, Mrs Rita Fan, regarded by many as unduly pro-China, in action. We should very much have liked to meet her but, not surprisingly, our request for an interview had been declined, due to her many commitments, although we were thanked for our interest and concern about Hong Kong. The meeting was full of problems, both the issues themselves and in the confusion of some members about what had already been said, or implied, by others. Mrs Fan missed nothing and her adroit handling of issues and people, her complete control of the whole procedure, was impressive.

Questions were asked about the outstanding debt the United Nations owed to Hong Kong in respect of the expense of the care and maintenance of the Vietnamese boat people and Vietnamese refugees stranded in Hong Kong, and whether the British government had been asked to take up the responsibility for solving these problems. The discussion was detailed and will not be recorded here but it is perhaps appropriate to mention that, while the remaining refugee situation was cited as being in part a legacy of the British government, the latter had also been generous, had worked closely with the authorities in Hong Kong and had taken thousands of refugees into the UK. Hong Kong itself had repatriated thousands of refugees or supervised their dispatch to other countries, having looked after them in Hong Kong until that time. The United Nations High Commissioner for refugees had indeed pressed for repayment of the debt by the UN but had been unsuccessful, mainly because of the cost of current troubles in Africa.

Hong Kong has not only provided land for the camps – and this a small Territory with its own disproportionately large population – but also paid out huge sums over the years, including an 'advance account', money formerly lent to the UN to pay the expenses of these new residents. Many Hong Kongers understandably believe they have done their bit. But a refugee problem remains for Hong Kong. Many believe the UN debt should be written off, others do not: some consciences are stirred, some hands are washed.

'An awkward adjustment for her.'

Born on the Chinese mainland, Yeuk-lam, eight years old in July 1997, was again living at her uncle's home in eastern Guangdong. She had been smuggled into Hong Kong aged about three months and had lived there until April 1997, when Immigration Department staff had taken her back to China. Yeuk-lam's mother said, 'It is an awkward adjustment for her. Here, villagers seldom speak Cantonese and the village is rather boring. She often asks to go back to Hong Kong.'

It is estimated that there were 66,000 mainland-born children in 1997 with right of abode in Hong Kong (with at least one parent resident in Hong Kong), but the rule was that application for permission to enter Hong Kong had to be made to mainland authorities, not to Hong Kong's own Immigration Department. The waiting period between application and permission, should it be granted, could be very long. Yeuk-lam's mother had made her application 11 years previously. She had waited for three years, heard nothing, and so smuggled her daughter into Hong Kong.

The new government of the SAR, facing an immediate flood of children surrendered by their parents to immigration officials after the handover, hurriedly passed a law saying that children in Hong Kong would be deported to the mainland unless they had a certificate of entitlement which had to come from the relevant authority in the mainland. Hence, Yeuk-lam's mother believed she and her daughter could be trapped there indefinitely.

Such cases aroused much anger and debate in the days immediately following the handover and, in particular, the retrospective nature of the new law came under heavy criticism. The children themselves were seen as victims of three political situations – China's restrictive emigration policy, Hong Kong's anti-mainland Chinese immigration policy, and the poor relations between Hong Kong's past and present sovereigns.

Much criticised, too, was the failure of the previous Legislative Council (under the British administration) to amend the Immigration Ordinance before July 1997 so as to prescribe the method by which these children could exercise their right to come to, or to stay in, the SAR. The law which gave the children right of abode in Hong Kong had been promulgated seven years earlier so that there had been, these critics argued, plenty of time in which to decide how these rights should be upheld.

At the same time, countered some officials, a large influx of children from the mainland would strain the provision of housing, medical and education services. Others in turn countered that such claims were an exaggeration and, even if they were not, the children anyway had the right to settle. Statements blaming them for aggravating Hong Kong's social problems were not conducive to their social integration.

In fact, there were many simultaneous conflicting responses to this desperate situation. Beijing came out with an announcement backing the new law which would, it said, provide a legal basis for the 'prompt repatriation' of the thousands of children who had entered the SAR illegally; in Hong Kong, a court battle loomed over the legality of the bill; independent newspaper surveys in Hong Kong suggested that four out of five people were in favour of imposing some measures to bar such children from claiming their rights by coming to Hong Kong illegally; the Bar Association and the Law Society of Hong Kong were both adamant that it was unconstitutional for the government to deny immediate residency rights to children from the mainland whose parents were permanent SAR residents; the new Chief Executive, Tung Chee Hwa, maintained that the new government's action *had* been in line with the Basic Law.

In the post handover days there were many newspaper articles and television programmes airing this immense problem, so pressing to so many in both a practical and an emotional sense.

'A burden on the community.'

Some other children had begun to experience difficulties earlier in 1997, although the latest source of their troubles lay in the coming change of sovereignty. Scores of young people with disabilities such as Down's Syndrome and autism, many of whom had previously lived at home, had been placed in hostels in Hong Kong because they had been abandoned by families seeking to emigrate to Australia, Canada, New Zealand, America and Britain who feared, usually rightly, that their applications could be debarred if they had dependants whose permanent care would be a burden on the adopted country's purse.

In March 1997, *The Times* reported this poignant situation, specifying the story of San who had been placed in a home two years previously, when her parents had left for Canada with her younger brother and sister. San had always lived at home and was by then a 21-year-old mentally handicapped woman. By day, the report said, she works in a sheltered workshop, packing plastic cutlery into polythene bags. She bitterly misses her mother and hopes she will come back.

Bing is another example. She had suffered a fever when she was two and has been mentally handicapped ever since. Aged 32, in March 1997, she had been left behind by her parents when they went to Canada.

Between 1988 and 1995, 434,000 people left Hong Kong, and an estimated further 90,000 may have left during 1996. There were no figures available for the handicapped people left behind in the Territory. Private hostels cost between £350 and £600 a month and Hong Kong welfare representatives fear that the family link will weaken and money for those left in such homes will no longer be sent. 'Taking care of these people will become a burden on the community,' said a member of the Hong Kong Society for the Relief of Disabled Children.

CHAPTER 16

TO DEPLOY QUICKLY
AND THINK ON THE HOOF

Every morning at 7am, three soldiers of the Black Watch raised flags at the Cenotaph in Central. Every evening at 6pm, they lowered them.

The poignancy of the soldier is that at the peak of his physical and mental strength he must be prepared to kill, and to die. The main peacetime task of the military is to train for such combat and the period January – September 1997 was designated a Black Watch Company level training period. On 30 April some men flew back to Scotland to fulfil duties there, many of them disappointed to miss the run-up to 30 June. But they did not miss the rigorous training in the Far East. In the words of Colonel Alasdair Loudon's Training Directive:

> We must take every opportunity we can to train while in Hong Kong. Indeed if we do not train efficiently we will be no use to anyone, least of all to ourselves ... I want us to train hard ...

In Hong Kong, evidence of past need for preparation for combat lay all around and, in 1997, all Black Watch troops toured battlefields of the Second World War, including Wong Nai Chung gap, where British casualties had been massive. Here the great-uncle of a currently-serving Black Watch corporal had been shot, aged 25, by a Japanese sniper, and lies buried in the military cemetery at Stanley, along with hundreds of

The last container is closed, Stonecutters' Island. BBC cameraman films. (Craig)

men and women from many parts of the Commonwealth. One headstone reads:

Capt. D. Ford. GC
18th Dec. 1943. Age 25
He won life for friends
This ground for Scotland
And glory for God.

Leading his men on their last training exercise in Hong Kong, Colonel Loudon told the BBC's Asia Correspondent, Fergal Keane, that the New Territories were a very useful training area. 'It's hot here, and you work very hard. It's not like the kind of training the men are used to at home.' The forests with their thick cover and wide streams provided an ideal testing ground. For more than a century British troops had trained in the area and Keane wrote:

'The crackle of rifles firing blank rounds, the roars of NCOs and the sound of men crashing through the thick undergrowth are all familiar to the farmers of the area.'

Exercises in February had taken place in foul pouring rain, cold, and a fog which was blowing in from the sea. Later, tasks were undertaken in searing heat, including a close-quarter battle down an overhung stream bed in the presence of a BBC team. 'A microphone picked up every shout, grunt and deep breath as they flung themselves behind cover or dashed through the water to the next fire position.'

Duties were to include border surveillance, practice at moving in and out of observation posts, their construction, the use of night viewing devices and slick radio procedure. High intensity scenarios for all practices were to be adopted at High Island Training Camp, where there was opportunity for concentrated and uninterrupted training: practice fire control, and restraint too, and all to be confident in firing all weapons within platoon and defence and attack tasks. Days on the ranges would culminate in a 36-hour battalion-controlled exercise to test company commanders' ability 'to deploy quickly and think on the hoof'.

In support of the Royal Hong Kong Police, several observation posts were used to identify illegal smuggling and the exercise resulted in the capture of a Chinese trading vessel involved in illegal smuggling of cars and electrical goods.

The Royal Hong Kong Police also provided ranges for sniper practice

Rehearsals,
Stonecutters' Island.
June 1997. (Craig)

– judging distance and observation are two very hard skills to master. The sniper has to establish 'whether the enemy is standing at 600m or 1000m over undulating ground, therefore adjusting his sights to ensure he can achieve a one-round kill.'

A surprise was in store for some residents of the Sai-Kung area when a company on training exercise finished with a large ambush on the High Island Dam, which somewhat disturbed the local hippie community.

There was also training for promotion to Junior Non-Commissioned appointments. Everyone was to take part in at least three fitness periods a week. Discipline was to be of the highest order.

It all looked rather like taking down the Christmas decorations on Twelfth Night, although in fact it was Friday, 13 June and there were still 17 days to go to the Big Day. Inside the Officers' Mess on Stonecutters', pictures which had been on the walls during the previous evening's music and reels, now lay on the floor or were propped up against table-legs and chairs. The last of the silver was being carefully wrapped.

This was the morning following the Beating Retreat supper, and the military possessions were being packed up and made ready for send-off. Some members of the press witnessed these scenes and a BBC camera man muttered as he filmed the last crates disappearing into the back of a lorry bearing Chinese number plates that the exercise had begun earlier than scheduled. Other crates marked with red crosses were prepared and a drum disappeared into its own round box. All this was part of fulfilment of duties in support of the closure of the 156-year-old garrison. Somehow, these final moments of military possessions at Stonecutters' were especially memorable and, after that morning, all that remained was personal baggage and plastic cutlery.

The next week, military bands arrived, flown in especially for the final military parade. For the next two weeks, Stonecutters' was a colourful, lively, tuneful place – drilling, Pipes and Drums and Band rehearsals, and more drilling, Pipes and Drums and Band rehearsals. These new arrivals meant that some 500 people had to be fed daily. Much of the kitchen equipment had been sold and the German airline,

Lufthansa, provided meals for the whole garrison for the final week.

There were other demands upon battalion resources: its chefs were very popular at civilian events, and the training cycle was officially broken between 17–24 March so that soldiers could assist at the Hong Kong rugby 7s and 10s, international seven- and ten-a-side competitions. Black Watch mechanics were also kept busy because the remaining vehicles were old and resources were very limited due to the drawdown of spares. But all servicing was up-to-date right to the end.

In constant demand were the Pipes and Drums at all kinds of functions, civilian as well as military, including the opening of the Tsing Ma Bridge, the Old Etonian Dinner and the Caledonian Charity Ball. The Highland Band twice Beat Retreat at the house of the Commander British Forces, reported by several to have been memorable occasions.

Just before the handover, a small private party, hosted by David Tang, one of Hong Kong's richest entrepreneurs, was held for the Governor. Black Watch Pipers appeared suddenly out of the darkness, playing, amongst other tunes, *Highland Cathedral*, a favourite of the chief guest.

One of the busiest departments. Keeping the battalion mobile with an aged fleet and limited resources is not an easy task.

(Frank Proctor)

Earlier in the tour, a dramatic Beating Retreat for Officers' and Sergeants' Messes, and their guests, was held on Stonecutters' Island. The event is vividly described in the *Red Hackle – Chronicle of the Black Watch*:

In order to make it that bit different, the Pipe Major planned a gathering of the Clans in a small but steep bowl which lies on the island and at which the mess marquees were laid out. The Clans came from D Company and were summoned by bugle and pipe calls from the surrounding hills, to rally around Faichney's Castle. As the calls sounded in the dark, Clan Delta were seen bearing flaming torches, coming off the hills and out of the woods into the glen, before rallying on the flanks of the Castle. Once the calls were complete and with the stragglers still moving to the gathering, we burst from the gates of Castle Faichney. The effect was extremely impressive and more than one guest was heard to remark that the final Beating Retreat in June will have to be an Andrew Lloyd-Webber event to beat this one.

View of band rehearsals from the Officers' Mess Balcony, Stonecutters' Island. (Craig)

Hectic rehearsals – too little time with such a large number of bands – to prepare for the programme of military music at the Hong Kong Stadium. For many, this was the final 'live' military farewell, for attendance at the military parade on 30 June was by allocation. Stadium tickets were free but almost ran out on the first day they were available. The packed Stadium included thousands of Chinese, many of whom wept, as well as Ex-pats and dignitaries, amongst whom were Governor Patten and the Head of the Civil Service, Mrs Anson Chan.

Under the direction of Lieutenant Colonel David Price, music was played by the Scots Guards, the Highland Band, the Royal Marines, The Pipes and Drums of the 1st Battalion the Black Watch, and the Brigade of Gurkhas. 'We have innumerable memories of shared experiences,' wrote the Commander British Forces in his foreword for the programme, 'good times and bad, but, predominant in those memories is the happy, good-natured relationship with the people of Hong Kong of all races.'

Lt Col David Price rehearses on Stonecutters' Island. (Craig)

Patient Gurkha drummer endures 1 ½ hour over-run during early civilian rehearsal of Farewell Parade. (Craig)

CHAPTER 17

NEVER HAVE PEOPLE
BEEN SO MISINFORMED

When the advance guard of the PLA arrived, those designated to the Prince of Wales Barracks were assigned to Blake Block, the north side of which faced the harbour. For a time, British troops barracked there, too, and the doors into the PLA quarters were kept locked. A PLA flag appeared, and a notice announced the area out of bounds, except to PLA troops. On Stonecutters', the early PLA arrivals lived in the west end of the island and, along with oral instruction, geographical distance made a clear enough demarcation.

Front entry to the Prince of Wales Barracks that was closed off for two weeks during July 1997. (Craig)

Prearranged parties brought together small numbers of officers of both armies, but the rest of the time the British and Chinese were kept apart, to pre-empt difficulty rather than as a symptom of ill-will. At POWB, in the latter period, there were at times some bullish feelings – at least on the British side – 'it didn't feel right' and 'we were fed up, it felt like confrontation with the enemy'. The general policy was clearly directed towards maintenance of mutual respect and goodwill but here the combination of close physical proximity and strict demarcation did provide some tension but without causing damage on either side.

During the last two weeks of June the political temperature in Hong Kong was raised by a sudden demand from the Chinese side, that a further advance batch of PLA troops enter the territory a few hours before midnight on 30 June. All the way through the military negotiations it had been assumed, at least by implication, that after the third advance batch, which arrived on 30 May, no further Chinese troops would arrive before 1 July. The advance troops who did arrive early were unarmed and deemed essential to reasonable logistical preparation for the main contingent. This unexpected demand, which put strain upon what had been until then a constructive, on the whole civil, relationship between the negotiating British and Chinese generals, threatened the smooth run-up to transition.

Major General Dutton's letter of congratulation to Major General Liu Zhenwu upon his appointment as commander of the Hong Kong garrison, and his subsequent visit to Shenzhen, the first of a CBF, Hong Kong, to mainland China, were acts of imaginative and diplomatic flair and had got things off to a good start. They were, too, gestures in striking contrast to the political parallel, with Governor Patten and the leaders and officials in Beijing arriving early at the point when they neither spoke nor visited, each other.

The three advance parties of the PLA had come into Hong Kong quietly. Major General Dutton had welcomed the first batch: 'We will be working hard together to achieve our common purpose, the smooth transfer of defence responsibility for Hong Kong.'

Major General Zhou Borong, leader of the advance PLA troops,

PLA sentries in best uniforms, Prince of Wales Barracks. (Craig)

responded: 'Our work will enhance the understanding and co-operation between the two sides. This is very important.'

The two subsequent advance arrivals, though not marked by speeches, had the same purpose. Meetings between some members of both armies had followed – professional, to organise details of the transition, and social, for goodwill. To many, the idea of a minor PLA presence seemed practical and sensible. A British Joint Liaison Group official said: 'After all, you can't simply expect these guys to walk in not knowing what lights to switch on and nothing in the refrigerator.' The late surprise demand which cut into this reasonable state of play had come not from Chinese military in Hong Kong or Shenzhen, but from Beijing. The British ultimately agreed to the earlier arrival – about 9 o'clock in the evening of 30 June – of a further small number of PLA troops. But under no circumstances would the last British troops move out before midnight.

On 1 July, a burst of thunder marked the entry of the last vehicle bearing PLA soldiers across the border into Hong Kong. They headed for one or other of the military sites prepared for them by the advance parties across the Region. Open trucks carried soldiers standing erect on the decks, wearing green uniform and white gloves, and carrying high across their chests weapons that gleamed. The troops were greeted by dragon-dancing, flag-waving, cheers and flowers as, simultaneously, the rain poured down and soaked their uniforms.

Within this dramatic entry lay a paradox: while some Hong Kong citizens feared the PLA's arrival as a threat to their own way of life, it was, in reality, an embodiment of tension and power-play in Beijing. In Hong Kong, the Chinese army was seen as the agent of a political system which was polarised from their own, and inimical to it – a Communist system. For some citizens this was a system from which they had already fled:

> My father is a bit frightened. That's because he came to Hong Kong to escape the Communists. That experience still scares him. Anything to do with the Communists, especially the PLA, will frighten.

For people such as these, the words of the Chief Executive designate on the eve of the handover, that the troops were 'very well disciplined' and

Entering Stanley Fort.

August 1997. (Craig)

once the Hong Kong people got to know them 'they will become part of our community' must have fallen on very stony ground. Nor, for them, would reassurance be found in his words on American television, which stressed that the PLA troops could not move against Hong Kong people without his approval – 'they will not, they cannot'.

But others, not so traumatised, could see hopeful signs: 'Things are changing here and China has changed too. There's no way to turn the clock back.'

A different point was made by the leader of the Democratic Party, Martin Lee, who believed it was not necessary for Chinese troops to be stationed in the territory because it could be adequately defended from the military base just across the border from Shenzhen. But these last words suggest a misreading by Martin Lee of the message, as intended. For the propaganda publicity accorded to the PLA's arrival into Hong Kong was not so much about the defence of the Region as a move to further consolidate the power of the new leadership in Beijing. Reunification provided its own variation on the theme of the army as the principal force by which Chinese leadership acquires and holds onto, power. Mao Zedong and Deng Xiaoping had come to political ascendancy with the support of the military, but Jiang had to woo it, and the happy event in Hong Kong, the end of a century and a half of humiliation, was an opportunity to please the Chinese generals as well as to feed the political propaganda machine. The recovery of Hong Kong, the sovereignty over which was represented by the arrival of the PLA, was a feather in the cap of the Beijing leadership, in particular of President Jiang, and as much mileage as possible was to be made out of it.

The Hong Kong contingent, the cream of the Chinese army, was hand-picked as a show force, above all intended to impress the Chinese mainland population and the rest of the world. Beijing's intention was not to strike fear into the hearts of the Hong Kong people, although sections of the international press strove hard sometimes to make it seem so. This was a pity from the point of view of the PLA troops established in Hong Kong. General Liu Zhenwu had said publicly before the handover that he hoped the presence of the army in Hong Kong – an opportunity for it to earn respect – might help erase associations made with Tiananmen Square. But much of the press gave little publicity to this statement, some even writing of the PLA's arrival as having grotesque intentions for Hong Kong.

This was wholly irresponsible for although it is true that the Chinese army itself conducts its affairs, compared to the British, with a lack of transparency, and the government in Beijing does not encourage the publicising of accurate information about the army's organisation and function, there was enough information available for it to be known that, in current Chinese military circles, there is a determination for the PLA to become a professional army and that it is already an army undergoing significant transition.

Instead of stimulating circulation by concocting sensation and fanning fear, the press could have enlightened readers about this military move forward and away from the days of Tiananmen Square This might also have spared those inhabitants of Hong Kong, asleep in their beds in the middle of their night, from telephone calls from relatives in other parts of the world, counselling flight from Hong Kong or, if they were mad enough to remain, at least to stay indoors.

Amongst all this fear, genuine and falsely generated, there lay a sharp poignancy. For some of the arriving Chinese soldiers, too, held misgivings and were themselves nervous, perhaps frightened even, of the crowds who had come to watch them as they entered Hong Kong and were as full of apprehension, as some of their observers, that they had come to stay.

The following are intended to demonstrate the sadder aspects of reporting and speculative writing, which made a significant impact upon opinion in Hong Kong and the UK as both awaited the arrival of the People's Liberation Army. Allusions, both implicit and explicit, to Tiananmen Square 1989 and the overall tone when mentioning the Chinese Army are instructive.

The fear that turns China's leaders into bullies.

Security is an obsession with the Chinese leadership ... It is merely a question of keeping the (Communist) party in power. Hence the importance of the PLA, today just as much as eight years ago when it shot down demonstrators in their hundreds.

And also:

> …. it is never entirely comfortable to be too close to China. The more troubled it is at home, the more angry and manipulative it is abroad. An insecure autocracy is a difficult autocracy, and the Chinese Communist Party has reason to be extremely insecure. Not surprisingly, therefore, President Jiang Zemin wants the PLA to be on hand for his big moment tomorrow night. He feels safer that way.
>
> John Simpson, BBC World Affairs Editor. *Sunday Telegraph.*
> 29 June 1997

Ignoring the irony, the same newspaper had, on another page, Simon Winchester:

> ... Even after Tiananmen Square, old generals and brigadiers in the PLA would talk to Clare Hollingsworth – the distinguished Hong Kong journalist - trying to explain themselves to one of the few western journalists who tried to see them as professional soldiers and not merely as puppets of a cruel regime.

Another article, same newspaper, same day. Again Simon Winchester:

> The ceremony that will come in time to mean very much more (than the handover) to the average Chinese in Hong Kong is the one that will in fact happen tomorrow, and each and every day at dawn, 2,000 miles north of here in Beijing ... each day's raising of the great red flag of Communist China ... The six and a half million people who live here are now about to undergo a process of being cajoled, persuaded – and perhaps even bullied – into accepting that they are

Chinese through and through, and that their spiritual centre is now and for ever more in and around the Celestial Throne, in the Forbidden City, in faraway Beijing.

... The Chinese People's Liberation Army is clearly going to be one of the instruments by which the Beijing leadership intends to bring the ordinary, very independently minded Hong Kong citizen to heel. Friday's announcement of the speed and size of the army's deployment suggests the urgency with which China is about to begin the process of the Sinicisation, or the patriotic re-education of Hong Kong.

Four thousand troops will stream in at dawn on Tuesday, by land, sea and air, in a steady cavalcade of armoured cars, helicopters and naval vessels ... There can be little doubt that they are being sent to Hong Kong in such numbers and with such speed ... to help instill in the Hong Kong people politically correct thoughts and attitudes, and a fervent love for the motherland.

And for the future?

Only officials who are infinitely more doctrinally loyal than those in place today will get the nod. And, once installed, their impact on the territory will be far harsher than is being promised during these heady, internationally scrutinised handover days, continued Simon Winchester in the same article.

Jonathan Mirsky, commenting on an informal conversation between Generals Dutton and Liu, said in *The Times*, 24 February 1997:

According to General Dutton, General Liu assured him that 'the Chinese wished to use Hong Kong as a window on the world ...' General Liu's observations are the first public admission by a Chinese military man and, perhaps, any senior official that the Tiananmen massacre nearly eight years ago was anything more than the army putting down a 'counter-revolutionary uprising'.

In fact, General Liu had admitted nothing of the kind – no mention of a 'counter-revolutionary uprising' even, and certainly none of massacre. All General Liu had said was that he was concerned that 'Tiananmen Square' was ... 'the image the world had of the People's Liberation Army' and that 'the Chinese wished to use Hong Kong as a window on the world to reverse that image'. This article concluded: 'The garrison will number about 10,000'. (It actually numbers 4,000 – maybe less.)

Two further vignettes of the media making the message. The first was in *Newsweek*, 19 May 1997. Harry Wong, described as 'one of Hong Kong's most multi-talented media personalities' said:

> I do a comedy talk show for a Chicago radio station called *Count Down to Communism*. They ask me things like: "So have the tanks rolled in yet?" or "Are there opium dens in Hong Kong?" It's shown me just how little Americans know about Hong Kong and China. All they know is Tiananmen from CNN.

Secondly, Simon Jenkins wrote in *The Times*, 30 June 1997:

> The weather is horribly hot and humid. Black clouds have spent the past day massing menacingly over the distant Chinese mountains, as if ready to pounce.

General Liu Zhenwu told his troops before they crossed the border:

> I hope you will conduct yourselves and abide by the laws so as to establish for the Hong Kong garrison the reputation of a powerful and civilised force. You must love the people of Hong Kong ... and with your actual deeds win the support and love of the Hong Kong people. You should be civilised and courteous. You should also forget about fame and fortune. I hope you can bring justice into full play to resist all kinds of evil winds and noxious influences. We must ensure

that our troops can withstand the tests of special circumstances and complicated situations.

Not much publicity was given to that address in the world media.

On 9 July, General Liu Zhenwu welcomed the new Chief Executive of Hong Kong, Tung Chee Hwa, and a select group of officials to Stonecutters' Island, now the new PLA navy base:

> We shall not interfere in the internal affairs of the Hong Kong Special Administrative Region.... we shall not create troubles for the Hong Kong government. We shall respect Hong Kong's way of life and the rule of law.

Press reporting on the Hong Kong handover clearly underlines one major question of the hour – how far down the road are we prepared to go towards the point where the media negotiates, and ultimately even becomes, our reality?

Do we agree or disagree with the distinguished Hong Kong financier who said to us of the press coverage: 'Awful. Never has more information been available ... never have people been so misinformed'?

CHAPTER 18

I'M SURE THEY'RE NOT
HERE TO DEFEND US

A week after the handover, late in the day, we visited Emily Lau, recently established in a new office in Central. She had left behind her room in the Legco Building, having been along with other elected councillors, thrown out of office on 1 July to make way for the new Provisional Legislature. In the 1995 elections, she had been returned for

Group of Filipinas –

Central. (Craig)

New Territories East, polling the highest number of votes in the 20 directly elected geographical constituencies, and in the 1991 election she was the first and only woman directly elected. One of Hong Kong's most popular politicians, she had accused Mrs Thatcher, then UK Prime Minister, in public and to her face, of betraying six and a half million Hong Kong people.

The PLA were now established in Hong Kong, and much anxiety had been fuelled by lack of information about how many Chinese troops were eventually intended for the garrison and the precise parameters of the PLA's right to interfere in the life of the new SAR. Even more alarming, some thought, was the knowledge that, unlike the British Governor, who had always been Commander-in-Chief of the garrison, the new Chief Executive had no such authority – and worse, Beijing retained the authority. Might the army one day be used to crush Hong Kong's way of life? And what if PLA officers accidentally lobbed a bomb on a civilian residence? Would the victims have to sue the PLA in a mainland court instead of appealing to the local judiciary? There had been earlier alarm about the draft PLA garrison law which held that Hong Kong courts could only try criminal charges against military personnel if they had been committed when the defendant had been off-duty. Such matters were being hotly debated at the time we saw Ms Lau, not least in Kevin Sinclair's article published that day in the *South China Morning Post*.

> Grim-faced PLA soldiers goose-stepped across the front pages of London newspapers. The message was inescapable; watch out, Hong Kong, because here come the bloody-fanged villains of Tiananmen Square. What nonsense ... 'They are coming by land, by sea, by air,' wailed former Legislative Councillor Emily Lau ... It may have escaped the notice of Ms Lau and much of the international press, but sailors tend to get about by sea, aviators often fly and soldiers travel by land.

Ms Lau told us she had been dropped out of press reports, although there had been mention of her in an article that morning: 'I am frozen out, not reported in the Hong Kong press even; what I say they don't want to know or write. I am trouble.'

Ms Lau: feisty, bottled up, angry, close to tears even, and a clear contrast to the collected, poised, witty Martin Lee; like him articulate, but rather in the manner of a scalded cat than of a cool counsel incisively slicing to expose the truth. Her outspoken anti-China stand had led to this side-lining in local newspapers in which, she believed, self-censorship had already come to stay. We asked her about the British Prime Minister, Tony Blair:

> I have no hope or optimism in the British Government – let's talk about the British Government in general, as a whole. They will do nothing for us. America, France, Germany – they will do nothing for us.

Secretary of State Albright had said to her; 'you should know your friends'.

> Tsch! What a cheek, I am sick of these people ... Akers-Jones and ... others, they are creeps. They did well under the British government, now they want to do well under China. I'm sick of them. I don't care about them. Mrs Thatcher is terrible, yes. She betrayed us. The British government is betraying us now as well.

Ms Lau, like Martin Lee, condemned the Provisional Legislature now established in the Legco Building:

> Not legal. How can it be? It is contrary to the joint Declaration and the Basic Law. Beijing can't say 'we say, therefore ...' It will be OK if China's perception is that things here are under control. If not, they will crack down on us, as in Beijing. The PLA? I don't know about them [still no mention of Sinclair's article] but I'm sure they're not here to defend us.

What did she think of the new Chief Executive? 'Tung – I told him, we don't do things like that.' In his first week of office he had visited the PLA at their naval base on Stonecutters' Island but only the Beijing media had been present; the local press had not known of the visit until it was over and they heard about it in reports from Beijing. And the last Governor?

Patten? The best Governor we've had but that's not saying much, they've been so awful. He answered questions and made the administration more accountable. That is good. I lost my bill for full democracy the day Patten won his bill for limited democracy. We should have got democracy decades ago but we didn't. Better what came in 1992 than nothing. Not too late, but too little. Martin Lee's vote made me lose mine.

Ms Lau handed us a copy of her talk of 6 July on *Radio Hong Kong*. In it she had said her piece about the PLA, so ridiculed by Sinclair. But it was not just the PLA who were in her sights.

In the case of Britain, a country which has run Hong Kong for 156 years, many people believe the British government would not lift a finger to help us should we get into trouble. Like many other governments, London's top priority is getting a slice of the huge China market. We have also not forgotten that trade was the reason why the colony of Hong Kong was founded in the 19th Century … It is remarkable that the transfer of six million free people into the hands of an authoritarian regime was concluded without bloodshed or violence. The main reason for the lack of resistance was that many Hong Kong people regard themselves as Chinese. Moreover, they were overwhelmed by the feeling of helplessness before the might of the Chinese Communist giant. Many protected themselves by securing foreign citizenship or right of abode in democratic and free countries.

Another target:

> A handover hotline for students set up by the Catholic Church found that 60 per cent of the callers were opposed to unification with China. The students also complained about getting poor marks from their teachers because they voiced objection to Chinese rule in essays on the handover. Conversely, students who sang the praise of unification got full marks.

Before we left we asked Ms Lau for her views on Jonathan Dimbleby and his book *The Last Governor*, just published, and on sale in Hong Kong.

> Jonathan Dimbleby – he interviews everyone here each year. He likes them to say something different next time so he can say they've contradicted themselves. But not me. I've been saying the same thing. Patten even said I have never been wrong. For ten years I have said what will happen, and got it right.

Flowers in D'Aguilar Street. Hong Kong.

(Craig)

CHAPTER 19

IT IS TO US THAT THE PEOPLE IN HONG KONG WILL LOOK

'What then of the future?' wrote Police Commissioner Eddie Hui Ki-on in his foreword to the 1996 *Royal Hong Kong Police Review*. 'As we move into a year of transition, our contribution to the future success of Hong Kong is essential. The importance of the role which every member of the Force has to play in ensuring that Hong Kong remains a safe, law abiding, stable society cannot be underestimated. It is to us that the people in Hong Kong and those overseas will look for confidence.' And indeed one cannot underestimate the importance of the part the Police Force plays in the unique territory that is Hong Kong.

Because of the odd combination of circumstances – British administration, Chinese hard work and business acumen – the territory evolved in such a way that it acquired the main benefits of full democracy without actually having anything like that full democracy on the statute book. Indeed, it functions in a way which should be the envy of many Western governments. It has the rule of law, freedom of speech, an independent judiciary, freedom of assembly, an open market and thanks to the Police Force, an enviable record of law and order; and this in a complex, bustling cosmopolitan society. A happy state of affairs, which was not reached, of course, without hazard and, as with Hong Kong, the history of the Police Force is a series of crises sparked off by external events, both Chinese and international.

In 1946, just when the reforms initiated by Duncan MacIntosh, the post-war Commissioner, increasing numbers and improving rates of pay and housing were bearing fruit and he could begin to make an impression on the sorry state of Hong Kong, the climax of the Communist-Kuomintang civil war sent a million refugees pouring in over the Shenzhen River and from Shanghai. Unfortunately, amongst their numbers, there were many battle-hardened Kuomintang veterans who were angry and dangerous in defeat. Policemen were ambushed and killed just for their revolvers, kidnapping was common and there was endless violence. Precautionary fortified posts – still known as MacIntosh cathedrals – were built along the 32-kilometre stretch of border, from which the police could observe Communist soldiers taking over checkpoints on the other side. Though surrounded by paddy fields and fishponds, giving it the tranquil air of traditional southern China, it has often been a turbulent and dangerous area. In 1962, for instance, China, without warning, withdrew its army and police units and, as a natural consequence, tens of thousands of its citizens swept south over the rivers to be caught and returned home.

Incidentally, during this period, every one of the then 273 women in the Force was rushed to the frontier because their presence helped to

A watch tower along the
S.A.R. border. (Craig)

control any panic in the great surging masses. There are now 3,160 women throughout the Force, and the Regional Commander New Territories North is a woman.

Until 1980 most of those arriving were allowed to stay, provided they had reached the urban areas. Since then, however, with the territory bulging at the seams, China and Hong Kong have agreed that all those arriving illegally should be repatriated. And, of course, those paddy-fields now house a mini-mirror-image of Hong Kong. Luckily, Commissioner MacIntosh's improvements were good enough to withstand all this upheaval and the crises that followed.

On Christmas Day 1953 a huge fire amongst refugee shacks at Shek Kip Mei made 58,000 homeless which led to Hong Kong's amazingly successful public housing programme. These early basic resettlement buildings were soon filled with new arrivals from China, many of whom were Kuomintang. When in 1956 a Resettlement Officer pulled down a Kuomintang poster on Nationalists' Day (10 October), angry protests led to vicious rioting in which gangsters gleefully joined.

This led to the formation of what was to become the Police Tactical Unit (PTU). At its HQ in Fanling, thousands of serving police officers

Amiable demonstration

at Legco. July 1997.

(Craig)

173

are trained in riot control and techniques aimed at public protection with the minimum use of force. Units are sent to serve in a region from where they can easily be deployed as required. Their first test was the Star Ferry riots, resulting from a small fare increase. There was no warning; one night the streets were as usual, the next mobs rioting and looting. An even greater test came in 1967 when the Mainland Cultural Revolution led to riots, bombings, and disruption. The PTU passed with flying colours.

Police pay in Hong Kong was traditionally low even compared with that of other public servants, and there were serious flaws in management. It was common knowledge that corruption though never publicly admitted was endemic in both the Police Force and the community, so the new Commissioner, Charles Sutcliffe, began widespread reforms against great opposition. He changed the rank structures and, after a full review, increased pay. The discovery of one Chief Superintendent's accumulation of an enormous fortune rocked Hong Kong and led to the formation of the Independent Commission Against Corruption which had considerable powers.

In 1977 the police protested that they were being victimised by the anti-corruption drive and the government, feeling that enough was enough, issued an amnesty. Obviously, this was a very painful period for the Force but, again, it resulted in a big step forward. Most young policemen were glad to move on into the future and when a Commission finally suggested a realistic living wage, the Hong Kong Police Force we see today was on its way – better manned, more accountable and better directed.

Many of those reaching senior ranks in the early 1980s were Chinese whose prospects had been steadily improving. This showed not only a sensible realisation that Hong Kong Chinese should command the Police Force after reunification in 1997, as agreed by London and Beijing, but the successful outcome of a far-sighted career structure begun decades earlier.

The border still needs constant vigilance. From 1979 Army Units (the Gurkhas) were stationed there to help the hard-pressed police but in

1990, with an eye on 1997, the Field Patrol Detachment (FPD) was formed and began to take back sole responsibility for the border. It consists of an HQ Unit and four Companies of PTU and provides 24-hour security. Obviously, its main purpose is to catch illegal immigrants. Most of them are young men looking for work in the booming construction industry but some are criminals and it is they who make policing the border such a lottery. I was taken in a PTU Land Rover along stretches of the border and shown some of their observation posts on a very humid day and was amused to be told the Land Rovers did not have air-conditioning because this would make their occupants too comfortable and the crews might not be as diligent as they ought. As it was, one was glad to get out from time to time, in spite of the plastic mini-fan plugged into the lighter socket which merely seemed to move the humidity around.

There are two fences, the taller of which is 3.5 metres high with a topping of rolled barbed wire on the Hong Kong side, with a roadway between along which the police patrol in small groups, in constant touch with their post, looking for anyone bent on making a quick dash. This looks difficult but, in 1996, some 5,308 illegals were arrested attempting it. The Inspector told me the average time to get through and over the

Police Landrover on border road. (Craig)

wires is 90 seconds and that, although razor wire is not used on humanitarian grounds, some of them when caught are 'slashed to buggery, poor sods'. Nonetheless, the percentage of illegals with records of multiple entry into Hong Kong increased from 59.7 per cent in 1995 to 63.6 per cent in 1996, showing that they could get regular work in Hong Kong and that the scars were worthwhile. To combat this the police have increased prosecution of employers who take on illegals. I was told of employers who would take on illegal workers, saying that they would be paid at the end of the month as their wages were security for good work and behaviour; then, on pay day, the employer would ring the police and report them as illegals. The police said they had to go and pick them up but hated doing it because they knew the factory owner was getting his labour for nothing. Now the law is changed and employers have to check that they are not employing illegals. But life is not easy even for those who do get through. Males from the Northern provinces are often found begging and females in prostitution. In the main, though, illegals come from Guangdong, the neighbouring province.

Sometimes landslips occur and dash great holes in the fencing, which gives a great opportunity to someone lucky enough to be in the area, though, as the police pointed out, the trip over the border is no sinecure. The scrubland through which you approach the fence is thickly overgrown, as is the hilly scrubland on the Hong Kong side, so it is not surprising that more illegals try to come in by sea.

There are thermal imagers mounted at strategic locations along the border, linked to Police Operation Rooms by means of fibre optic cables. This means movement along the border during darkness can be monitored from the operations rooms and this improves the FPD's effectiveness. I was shown a place in the fence where an illegal had cut his way through and which had been hastily repaired. Running right along the fence, just above the level of the hole, is a thin black cable, which sends a signal to the Ops room as soon as the fence is touched and, as it also indicates the particular section, the Ops room can alert the nearest police with minimum delay. The Hong Kong Police (Ex-pats and Chinese) I met were justifiably proud of their service though equally alert to the faults of the Force and with thoughtful opinions on all matters from Vietnamese refugees to their own place in Hong Kong society. For instance: 'If I were at a party and said in conversation I was a police officer ... down would come the shutters.' There were fairly savage comments about 'Jardine Johnnies' who had a good life and made a great deal of money because Hong Kong was a safe place, but had not the manners to acknowledge the debt. 'All they talk about is money and making money. Not good.'

They did not, as a whole, approve of Governor Patten but admitted that the forces of law and order, who have to pick up the bits, are seldom in step with 'liberal' thought. It is not in the nature of their job. They felt he was thinking too much of himself and too little of his role. He was the Governor so he should have worn 'that silly hat' on ceremonial occasions. The last Governorship was no time to change styles. What he felt didn't matter, he was representing Hong Kong. One told the local joke that 'the 50,000 voters of Bath had a choice, the six million Chinese in Hong Kong did not'. Patten seemed to know 'absolutely nothing' about Hong Kong or China. 'I've been here for 16 years and I'm just beginning to come to terms with the Chinese mind – they've a wonderful culture but a very different one.' The general view was he was either 'very badly advised or ignored good advice!'

These were officers, NCOs and policemen. Some leaving, some staying. The Chinese seemed more content. Hong Kong has become their country. The police had been planning for the handover for many years and all should go smoothly. But some warned that corruption was coming back. 'Not necessarily money but moral ...'

For example, there were two senior police officers who were, frankly, mentally unstable and should have been dealt with, but they provided 'hostesses' for senior police officers and so they were left alone. The Fire Brigade staff took things from bodies removed in their ambulances and firemen attending genuine fires were often bribed to spray water on nearby factories which were not in danger, so that the owners can claim damage insurance. There are links with triads. Of course, they say, everyone goes on about corruption in the police but it is elsewhere too, in the legal system and in government departments for instance, though it is the police who get all the stick.

Another member of the Force said, 'the middle echelons are good but, on the whole, these good ones will not get to the top. The Freemasons have too big a hold.' As for the Ex-pats, those from the Metropolitan Police are not good for the Hong Kong Police. 'There is a type. There must be something wrong in London.' There is also reportedly too much unnecessary violence. 'You can hear screams from cells from time to time. No need for it ... with a prisoner just in for petty theft or something.'
Emily Lau had said: 'The police are a bit more civilised now ... but the beatings are terrible.'

The first impression we got in Hong Kong was that there were plenty of police about – there were 27,716 on the roll at the end of 1996 – and that a traffic jam, an accident or attempted robbery brought them to the spot on foot, by motorcycle and by car within minutes. Both the MTR and Kowloon Canton Railway (KCR) are remarkably hassle free as a result of the police having been consulted at early planning stages and 'an innovative and pro-active policing approach'. The crime rate in Hong Kong is amongst the lowest in the world.

We thought the acid test for the Hong Kong Police came over the four-day reunification period when, with security very tight and the mass presence of the international media, tempers could easily become frayed and actions much more peremptory. But this did not occur – they passed with flying colours.

CHAPTER 20

VERY FEW PEOPLE KNOW
OF ALL THIS

On 27 March 1997, there had been a grand public auction of garrison possessions. The sale included 100 Land Rovers, trailers, buses, ambulances, trucks, cars, plant machinery, a complete medical centre, computer equipment, five diesel engines, radio studio equipment, barbed wire, sandbags, used tyres, fans, sheets, bedspreads, cutlery, furniture, gymnasium equipment and, described as 'the last two items to be sold by the British garrison in Hong Kong', two Rover cars, and a 45-foot day boat used by the Commander British Forces and unavailable until 30 June. It became the responsibility of 1st Bn. the Black Watch to prepare many items for sale.

All the remaining ranges and training areas in Hong Kong also suddenly became the responsibility of 1 BW and it was the Black Watch that tidied them up and handed them over to the Hong Kong government. This aspect of the Black Watch tour was largely unrecognised in all the press coverage that went with the handover. Once the majority of vehicles had been sold, the battalion became entirely reliant upon hired transport and ferries, including ferry transport between Stonecutters' and the East Tamar Parade ground for many parade rehearsals.

Major Jim Williamson, the Black Watch Quartermaster, had invited us to return to Stonecutters' Island to explain the complexities of the island handover. So, on 18 June he was waiting, his door wedged open not in welcome but to air the place on a blistering hot afternoon and, doubtless, too, so that he could keep an ear on what else was going on. In the corridor, a row of military jackets hung from a bar, and on his desk lay a thick file detailing the already-completed disposal of the High Island Training Camp at Sai Kung, in the North East of the New Territories. This file bulged with maps, plans, details of equipment, each building and its contents set down, even every key noted, dated 29 April and signed by all relevant parties, including Major Williamson. With only ten days to go as British territory, Stonecutters' was currently undergoing the same sort of merciless scrutiny and, that afternoon, so-called 'hazard' certificates were being typed up and relevant maps completed.

This was the second wave of documentation: nothing 'sensitive', nothing 'hazardous' was to be left *in situ* unless recorded as such for the PLA. Each item deemed a hazard would be detailed, explained and colour-coded on a specially designed map. Once completed, these certificates would be handed initially to the Defence Land Agent, Colonel Haynes, and would be given to the PLA on the last day. Falling into this hazardous category were big naval guns, used during the Second World War as sea cover; the power station to the west of the island, equipped

Familiar sight.
Stonecutters'.
June 1997. (Craig)

Quartermaster celebrates documentary handover. (Craig)

with flood lighting to halt the approach of enemy submarines; a net running between Stonecutters' and Hong Kong island also to thwart submarines; derelict buildings; diesel tanks; chemical stores; open water tanks; old demolition pits where explosives left lying around had been blown up; compressed and hydraulic systems.

An earlier stage in the folding-up operation had led to the first set of documentation – the 'clearance' certificates, a process begun on 1 April 1997 and completed on 10 June. To make certain nothing was overlooked, and for the sake of general order, the island had been broken up into nine administrative areas and searched systematically from the west across to the eastern shoreline: in each area everything had been checked, everything 'sensitive' noted. Nothing was to escape the record; every single thing was cleared or cleaned, as appropriate – land, buildings, including derelict ones; gun positions; baths; stools; keys. Some gun sites, it was plain to see, had not been cleaned for years. The clearance certificates duly signed by appropriate parties with copies given to each, were given to the Government Property Agency for safe-keeping until 30 June on which day they would be given to the PLA. An enormous hard-backed file housed copies of clearance certificates, though covering only four of the nine areas. After 10 June, the Q.M and his team had been moved on to the other work before completion of the 'hazard' certificates.

Stonecutters' was the last military area to be made ready in this way for the change of sovereignty and Major Williamson had supervised the same operation on other sites: in 1994, on an earlier tour, parts of Stanley Fort on the south coast of Hong Kong island, and, during the current tour, the other parts of this Fort; the nearby Stanley Services Boat Club; the High Island Training Camp in Sai Kung; the Lo Wu Camp and Range on the border with China, and at Castle Peak, a huge area used for firing positions.

As it happened, the evening of the last Black Watch Officers' Mess Party was the same day that the clearance documentation had been handed to the Defence Land Agent, so that although the island was still occupied by the British garrison, technically it was no longer their property. Very few people knew this, and certainly Major Williamson made nothing at all of it, but in reality it was one of the momentous days in the long drawn out, unceremonious and behind-the-scenes, exchange of sovereignty.

In the same Mess, a few days previously, a small group of officers of the PLA Advance Guard had been hosted at a dinner by a small group of Black Watch Officers, and this occasion, too, had closed with Beating Retreat. In the Black Watch Visitors' Book which those present on this occasion all signed, was the signature of an earlier visitor – Colonel David Rose – who had led the Black Watch against the Chinese People's Liberation Army at the Battle of the Hook in Korea, in 1952. Did sons of sons who fought on either side at the Hook meet in Hong Kong in 1997? We will almost certainly never know.

Two days before this visit to Stonecutters', Major Williamson had attended a luncheon – a feast, he called it – hosted by the PLA. He produced the lavish menu card and it was interesting to hear about the luncheon which was attended by military and civil servants of both nations. The table was attractively laid out and waitresses had been brought from China for the occasion. Both General Liu and General Dutton made good speeches. The young interpreter Captain, though quite a bit of English was spoken by most of the PLA, was very good indeed. The Chinese proved pleasant and generous hosts, with a sense of humour and there was an easy relationship between the Chinese and British officers. There were small cups of potent alcohol (Maotai?) and their hosts tried to get their guests to drink as much as possible. The food was delicious, the fish, including salmon coated with mustard, all uncooked. All the dishes in all the courses were to be tasted by everyone. The Shark's Fin Soup was very tasty.

Events on Stonecutters' Island on 30 June are detailed elsewhere but we should mention here that on a different day an unofficial barbecue was held by some Black Watch Officers for some PLA Officers and that the QM and his assistant produced barbecued bananas with butterscotch sauce as the former's favourite – a creamy mixture made with milk and melted Mars Bars – could not be produced. There were no longer any Mars Bars on Stonecutters' Island.

Sub-aqua is fun.

(Ben Wrench)

CHAPTER 21

PLANNERS LOOK AT MAPS
NOT PLACES

'The Shalotung Valley is like no other place in Hong Kong,' said Ed Stokes, photographer and environmentalist, as we trod carefully down the bamboo-lined track towards Cheung Uk village. Everything was dripping wet, the humidity was at record levels, and the mosquitoes were rampant.

'Anywhere in the world this area would be striking,' he went on, 'but in ever-changing Hong Kong it's quite astonishing.' He swung round

Edward Stokes. Cheung Uk village. (Craig)

and pointed. The area is surrounded by hills which cradle the valley and make it invisible from below and because of its isolation, it now has a unique eco-system. We gazed about us. Four small streams meander around, merging into one larger water which, in its turn, winds through grass, shrub and wood. 'It's the only unpolluted slowly flowing stream in the entire territory.'

We had rendezvoused earlier near the taxi rank at Central Star Ferry and motored northwards via Kadoorie Farm and Tai Po. Suddenly leaving the main road we turned up a rough track which seemed to be about to peter out at any minute. 'Warn me if you see any big pot-holes on your side – sometimes the corners get swept away,' Ed murmured as he blithely swept the car on up the pitted concrete.

'We got what I hope will prove a benchmark decision last November ... when the Advisory Council on the Environment made what just might be a final ruling.' He stamped on the brakes at my croaked warning, skilfully skirted a patch where at least a third of the road had side-shifted downhill and went on, 'But it's been sadly drawn-out and there's still work to do.'

We passed an old graveyard set back from the track, with its little open huts containing ancestral urns, and then parked where the track came to an abrupt end. Ed led off down a little soggy path. He told us that in 1979 there were three old Hakka villages in the valley but that two are now abandoned and that the one we were heading for has only two or three people left. He paused to point out a small snake in a puddle in the path.

'Anyway the villagers all agreed to sell their land to the Shalotung Development Company. In return the Company agreed to build "villa" homes for them.' Apparently, falling property values froze the scheme until 1986 and then further plans for an 18-hole golf course which included 31 hectares of adjacent Country Park land were rejected.

Turning a corner we came across an electric-cable pole, in the middle of nowhere, on which hangs a white banner proclaiming the joys of reunification in vivid red lettering, left there by ex-villagers now living in Tai Po. At this point the path turned downhill for a few hundred yards and reaches the edge of a large clearing. And there, in front of us, is the village, with its little temple draped with vines threatening to engulf it. Eerily, a red light glowed from within. There is complete stillness, and nothing stirs. Skirting the marshy pool outside the temple, we passed the first of the derelict houses, decaying but still sturdy, with furniture and possessions scattered inside, giving the impression of a sudden exodus. Peering through one door standing ajar, I jump at the sound of a vague stirring at the back of the main room. I have fleeting visions of unknown inhabitants, illegal immigrants or even spirits. The surroundings edge your mind towards such thoughts. But a second hasty glance shows it is merely my own reflection in an old, stained mirror on the far wall. My sigh of relief is cut short by a roaring bark which, in the confined space, sounds like a Chinese dragon. It's that atmosphere again.

Ed is out of the door like a leaping salmon and we are close behind. 'Probably quite friendly, but you never know … better get a stick.' His voice radiates calm. I grab a handy branch about the size of a baseball bat, as a large black and tan dog pads menacingly towards us. I wonder in passing whether the Black Watch motto *Nemo Me Impune Lacessit* covers hefty Chinese 'wolves'. A couple of snuffling puppies gambol

The red light still burns in the little temple in the village of Cheung Uk. (Craig)

out of a side alley, which explains some of the ferocity, and after a few more thunderous growls, the dog withdraws and, joined by its mate, glares at us from a distance.

'There's part of dinner,' Ed points unnecessarily as we pass an evil-smelling pile of roast-duck scraps. 'Wouldn't linger if I were you.' We didn't. And so it was right through the village. Neglected homes filled with the personal detritus that delineates our lives: a giant wok, pictures, ornaments, clothing, chopsticks, old photographs ... 'Look at this – it's Trafalgar Square for heaven's sake.' 'Yes ... it will be. And here's another with a Soho restaurant group.' And he holds up a faded snapshot of a dozen smiling faces.

Ed told us that about 30 years ago cheap rice imports began to ruin the rice-farming way of life here. Selling excess crops had been the villagers' major cash income. So the young and able left in their hundreds, then thousands, to work at sea or in UK takeaways. Many joined the Hong Kong Police, others various government agencies, and soon the villages were emptied. The school was closed in 1987 and most old people were persuaded to move down the hill to Tai Po or even to Hong Kong itself.

'Is there anyone left?'

'There's meant to be one old man and two old women but there doesn't seem to be anyone about. Must be somebody ... that stinking duck ... '

A few quick glances show what an idyllic site the original villagers had chosen and how relatively little effort would be needed to make things shipshape again; but not for golf courses, eight-storey apartment blocks and luxury houses.

'So what's happening to the place now?'

'Last year's amended plans were rejected after the legislators were bussed out to Shalotung and actually saw the site for themselves.'

'That's good, isn't it?'

'As far as it goes ... it still leaves the villagers and the developers in limbo and, frankly, bloody angry.'

We ask if there is a solution, and Ed says he thinks the government should 'reassume' the land, pay off the developer and the villagers and incorporate Shalotung into Pat Sin Leng Country Park. The money is there, he says.

'Well now that Hong Kong is Chinese again ... ?'

'Maybe ... let's take a look at the main stream. It's worth the effort.' We move on past the last house and into the distant trees, towards the sound of water. As we emerge from the wood Ed, turning, signals us back. 'It's a little embarrassing,' he says. 'The old man's there bathing in a pool. I'll go ahead. He's a bit deaf and my Cantonese isn't up to much ...'

He strolls quietly forward until the old man looks up and smiles – no fear and no annoyance, just quiet interest. He looks remarkably fit and trim standing there in the middle of the stream. Progress has passed him by and Hong Kong Central is light years away. We smile and wave as Ed talks to him but don't take a photograph; somehow it seems too intrusive.

As we retrace our steps Ed tells us more about Chan Chung-Ching, the old Chinese man. He's about 76 years old and, when young, was in Chiang Kaishek's Kuomintang. He fled his home and wife in the Pearl River Delta in 1950 and has never seen either since. 'That was in the aftermath of the civil war when it was only too easy to lose touch ...'
He worked in factories for a bit until the Shalotung villagers took him in. The young were leaving in droves as has been mentioned and he was hired to work the village vegetable fields. I supposed all the ecological fuss must have gone over his head, as an outsider, and thought what a great chat I could have had if only I had had some Cantonese.

We stop to admire the hillside Feng Shui wood, and wonder that the richness of the local fauna and grasses growing on the old paddy fields should attract such large numbers of birds, bats and insects: 'Dragonflies, of course and butterflies. And mosquitoes.'

'And perfect cover for illegal immigrants?'

'Yes ... they come trooping over the hills almost every day on their way from the border to the fleshpots of Tai Po.'

We asked whether Ed thought that, with reunification, people would feel more of a sense of belonging. Up to now, Hong Kong had always been a place to make a pile and then move on. Maybe now people would want to make the place their home and certain things would follow like education, housing and the care for the environment?

'Planning will have to change. There's too much linear thinking ... poverty of thought ... Take the pollution statistics for example. Measurements are taken on the rooftops not on the ground where the effects are worst. Planners look at maps not places.'

As we retraced our steps, Jo and I wondered aloud whether Ed was really a little pessimistic about the future. But he denied this, saying that if Hong Kong uses the energy and skill that changed its post-war society so drastically, it has the resources, technology and wealth to support a sustained environmental agenda. It could green its urban areas, preserve its countryside and reverse the degradation of the entire Pearl River Delta.

There is a chance that Edward Stokes's book *Hong Kong's Wild Places*, a detailed study of the ecology of the entire territory, might be translated into Cantonese. The SAR (Hong Kong) government says it is interested and concerned. I took one last glance over my shoulder as we climbed back up the hill out of the old village. The red light still burns in the little temple.

CHAPTER 22

BY YOUR BADGE
MEN SHALL KNOW YOU

Yet no man may assume honour, neither may he enjoy pride without that he be worthy of them ... By your badge men shall know you. By your loyalty, by your behaviour, and by your technical skill, they will judge you as men, and measure your efficiency as soldiers.

Major General LECM Peroune CB, CBE, at Lamjung Camp,
Malaysia on 23 September 1954.

Their regimental history, since that date shows the Queen's Gurkha Signals, like all Signals, too often the army's unsung heroes, have more than kept their side of the bargain. Beginning with the Malaysian Emergency, it has been the usual Gurkha story of enterprise, adaptation, initiation and the pursuit of excellence. They have also deployed in Nepal (for the first Nepalese general elections), Germany, Borneo, Brunei, Sarawak, Croatia, Bosnia, the Middle East (the Gulf War) and, of course, Hong Kong.

Sadly, as for other regiments, the end of the 1960s heralded a large reduction in the size of the Brigade of Gurkhas. The Signals did not escape the cuts and saw its strength drop from 1,170 officers and men to 415 by 1971. The *Newsletters* of the time tell of the great sadness as the men went home to Nepal on redundancy.

One Hong Kong innovation was Trailwalker, first started in 1981 by 246 Gurkha Signal Squadron as a 100 km endurance exercise over the

Maclehose Trail. Since those early days it has grown into Hong Kong's biggest sporting charity fund-raising event, sponsored by the Hong Kong Bank and jointly organised by Oxfam and the regiment. Well over HK$35 million has been raised for charity of which a third has been given to the Gurkha Welfare Scheme.

A few days before they were to leave Hong Kong we spoke to a Gurkha Signals Squadron Captain – Navindra Gurung – and the then RSM – Omparkash Gurung – who had each served in Hong Kong for over 20 years. Despite their long service there and all the many changes they had witnessed they were to miss the biggest change of all, reunification with China. Along with most of their colleagues they would be returning to England before the handover and if they wanted to see their own Pipes and Drums playing *Auld Lang Syne* it would have to be on UK television. And what, one wonders, were the feelings of the Gurkha Pipes and Drums as they piped us out of Hong Kong and themselves into uncertainty? Neither complained; some people had, on their behalf, but to no avail. 'We're soldiers. We do what we're told and that's it.'

They believe Hong Kong will be a difficult place to control from the internal security point of view – with its population density and high

Last remaining Gurkhas from Hong Kong Gurkha Signals Squadron. June 1997.

(Craig)

Royal Gurkha Regiment Pipes and Drums enjoy a break in rehearsals, Stonecutters' Island. June 1997. (Craig)

rise buildings – and think it vital for the Hong Kong Police and the PLA to keep strict control over the frontier and prevent a rush of illegal immigrants flooding an already overcrowded Hong Kong.

Certainly Hong Kong's citizens have felt safe with the Gurkhas keeping the peace on the border. It was notable that fewer people took part in the latest Maclehose Trail when civilian guards took over this traditional role. There has been a Gurkha presence in Hong Kong since 1949, and the island is now home to many Gurkha children, with around 50,000 working in the city, many at the new airport where they can, temporarily, make good money. As Nepal has no large industries of its own, Hong Kong is an attractive alternative and a more exciting way to live life above subsistence level. The RSM himself is due to retire and will shortly be returning to Nepal to live on a pension which, he said, would not be adequate. This is a grim prospect with high inflation and little prospect of a suitable job. Gurkha pay has been improved recently, but for serving soldiers only. Pensions have not been increased to keep in step.

What would they most like from Prime Minister Blair's new government? 'A good, sensible defence review,' was the joint reply, 'with plenty of consulting and listening ... and decisions based on *military* requirements.'

Gurkha Signals with radar equipment on top of Prince of Wales Barracks. June 1997.

(Craig)

The RSM was sure China had its 'contingency' plans for Hong Kong well organised and whether they would ever be brought into play would depend on international developments. Everyone wanted Hong Kong to work. He would like to return in the year 2000, by which time, he thought, things would have settled down, though there would be changes; and not necessarily for the bad.

'You follow what's in the ascendancy ... '

Gurkha soldiers have served in Hong Kong since 1949 and today their children, who have automatic right of abode in Hong Kong, form a considerable second generation workforce.

Life for most of the inhabitants of Nepal is still lived at subsistence level and a prized route to a better living is a career as a soldier. Men who were born in the hills of Nepal have formed part of the British army since 1814, serving all over the world in peace and in war, and are everywhere respected for their loyalty, courage and toughness. There is no soldier generally more loved and honoured than the Gurkha.

In 1991, the British government, as the result of an overall defence review, announced a cut in Gurkha strength from 7,500 to 2,500 by 1997. This disastrous situation for Gurkhas and their families was transformed,

Sergeant Ho Chi Kau, antenna rigger, works at Prince of Wales Barracks. (JSPRS)

for some, by opportunities in a new venture. For simultaneously with the cuts and the consequently available skilled pool of new labour in Hong Kong, the security services needed recruits to meet the multiple needs of the Territory, such as the guarding and supervision of the ever-multiplying reclamation and reconstruction sites, of factories, offices, businesses and other power houses of Hong Kong's stupendous economy, as well as the houses of the rich, especially those sited on the Peak, hotels, conference centres, and VIP services. A mobile patrol service was also required. To meet these urgent needs the Jardine Securicor Gurkha Services (JSGS) was formed, and the blue beret has been a familiar sight in Hong Kong ever since.

At JSGS Headquarters in Cheung Sha Wan we talked to distinguished ex-Gurkhas, and others who had come there by a different route, who clearly believe that they now had a good employer. Pay is better than in the British army; there is a humane response when genuine need for compassionate leave arises; free flights home to Nepal are speedily arranged, including 24-hour insurance cover, a much-appreciated benefit not usually on offer.

One ex-Gurkha had retired from army life ten years before and after five years had taken up a second career with the JSGS. He had not lacked a natural desire to return to his native Nepal, but there he would have been unable to earn enough to provide the higher education and training which his children could receive abroad. In Nepal personal contact and string-pulling were the only way up and with a 30-year absence abroad, he lacked these advantages. It would take Nepal a very long time, he said, perhaps a hundred years, to be able to provide the necessary training and experience for its people to acquire the sophisticated

Gurkha Signals do 'Kukri Drill' for Italian film crew. P.O.W.B. 1997. (Craig)

business acumen to match the trading profits achieved already by Indian businessmen. His own daughter, who was studying at a university in America, intended when she was fully qualified to return to Nepal, and hoped she would then be able to make a contribution to helping her country on its way.

Along with British and Chinese ex-military, and one lone ex-policeman, the ex-Gurkhas are thoroughly retrained for the new job. Based upon a hierarchical command structure, the JSGS is run along military lines, with practices and expectations with which all are familiar. But the JSGS also draws from more distant roots in Nepal, where the hard life of a poor hill people teaches men to act as a community and to pull together. The organisation is now developed throughout the Asia Pacific region and is currently being set up in Malaysia.

There was some sadness and disappointment amongst the ex-Gurkhas that some who had served in the British army faithfully, often for decades, had, at a stroke, been deemed redundant by the politicians, and that, once redundant, or at the point of retirement, would receive pensions so low as to make a return to Nepal where there was little chance of work, an almost intolerable prospect. In earlier years, ex-First World War veterans had returned to Nepal to work barefoot in the fields; others had had to walk hundreds of miles to collect a paltry pension.

The 1991 decision to cut the Gurkha strength seemed to demonstrate a singular lack of grace and only public outrage had persuaded the Ministry of Defence to change a plan to deprive Gurkha servicemen, in 1997, of married quarters in Britain. At JSGS it was remarked that while the press had interviewed serving Gurkhas during the handover period, none had thought to visit ex-Gurkhas. 'You follow what's in the ascendancy, not what's going down.'

Change of sovereignty was bringing changes to the Service itself. That morning a potential client had insisted that his contract with JSGS should be written in Chinese. This had been anticipated and would be catered for. But how would the new SAR government accept this organisation, made up mainly of ex-British soldiers?

CHAPTER 23

A QUESTION OF JUDGEMENT

In his early days as Governor of Hong Kong and on the verge of his first visit to China, Chris Patten addressed Hong Kong businessmen at a luncheon. To the amused applause of his audience, he likened himself to a groom going to see his prospective parents-in-law. It seemed a good analogy. A few days later, still before his visit to China, and without discussing with the Chinese what he was going to say, he announced his proposed changes to the electoral system. China was furious and soon refused to have any dealings with him.

'A good friend, the Governor, a valued customer with a particular fondness for the custard tarts,' the proprietor of the Tai Cheong Bakery said, and, no, after the handover they would not be taking down his photograph. People on the streets, too, were enthusiastic about the Governor. 'Genuine', 'a very nice man', 'he has really tried, every week he visits somewhere'. But to the Beijing leadership, he was 'a whore', 'a prostitute', 'a triple violator'.

So, a controversial Governor: we found so many bases, criteria, yardsticks, by which his performance was measured, such difference in viewpoint, judgement and inclination, that he seems to elude assessment so that you can say 'Here, that's the man!' Yet as the comments piled up – and usually there was little hesitation, the words came thick and fast – it did become possible to identify some recurring point, some discernible pattern, so that in asking a stranger what he thought of the Governor,

The Governor, Chris Patten's, favourite custard tarts are sold here. (Note the photos on the right). (Craig)

you came to guess that in the answer you might learn as much about the speaker as the subject.

'He made the government, the civil service much more open, accountable,' – a Democrat (in fact many people of many sorts said this);
'He came regularly to the Legislative Council to answer questions directly,' – an elected councillor;
'He strengthened the will of the Hong Kong people,'– Martin Lee;
'Decent, a good touch when he talked informally or spontaneously to people he met,' – a clergyman.

On the other hand:

'A disaster from beginning to end, didn't do a thing right,' – an accountant;
'Not popular at all, we'll be glad to see him go,' – a Chinese businessman;
'Grumpy, unhelpful,' – a British businessman;
'Disliked by the business community tremendously,' – a financier;
'Clueless about military matters ... he had to be prodded to take the salute at the farewell Tamar ceremony' (and this about the Hong Kong

Commander-in-Chief), – words here spoken by a non-military man.

Not simply controversial, this Governor then, but a catalyst, a temperature-raiser, much liked or much loathed.

His appointment, too, some said, had been a foolish one; he was not the right man for the job. Nor was all the criticism of the appointment upon personal grounds: some believed it would have been wiser to put a diplomat rather than a politician into this tricky situation, especially during the run-up to a change of sovereignty, not from Empire to former colony, but from one nation to another, and particularly when one nation involved was China with its record of brutal, unrepentant intransigence. The best solution might have been to extend the contract of the previous Governor, Sir David Wilson, who had played a crucial part in the detailed work on the text of the Sino-British Joint Declaration. A former British ambassador to China, Sir Percy Cradock writes in his book *Experiences of China*:

> 'He [Wilson] was highly intelligent, a first-class Chinese speaker ... and had in addition that feel for the workings of the Chinese mind which I regarded as the negotiator's irreplaceable attribute. He had had experience as the China desk officer in the Far Eastern Department, as Editor of *The China Quarterly* and as Political Adviser in Hong Kong.

These qualities seem appropriate to the run-up to transition. An alternative might have been the appointment, for the last two years only, of a Governor who had not been involved in tricky negotiations with the Chinese, but who would confine his duties to carrying out the more ceremonial aspects of the office in the months before the handover. But, if the appointment had to be a politician and not a diplomat then one more consensual, less confrontational, would have better fitted the bill, someone (to leave out the living) more like Sir Alec Douglas Home, perhaps.

But Patten brought more specific personal disadvantages to the job, too. He came from a Westminster Parliament which, over the last two

The Convention Centre in preparation for 30 June 1997 Handover Ceremony. (Craig)

decades, had become increasingly confrontational in performance, and his career has been in the most didactic of party political stables. 'He was not entirely new to the joys of locking horns with Margaret Thatcher, when he first joined her Cabinet,' writes John Cole in his book *As It Seemed To Me.* As head of the Tory Research Department, over the years Patten had helped draft Mrs Thatcher's conference speeches and 'his own attitudes and those of his Prime Minister had always diverged widely'. Patten found her approach to European policy 'visceral' and, when he was her last Environment Secretary, he used to speak of her 'unbending and exotic will'. Perhaps, too, Patten had thought that nothing made much difference to the way Thatcher behaved? Anyway, inevitably the question presents itself, did his former experience of intimate dealing with one whose will was so inflexible and whose mind so closed to rational persuasion, better qualify, or render less suitable Chris Patten for the job of last Governor of Hong Kong? All his experience may seem to fall into the category of useful practice. On the other hand, his critics might say, an approach softer than the provocative one he was to adopt might in the end have gained, or at least retained, more democratic procedure for Hong Kong after 1 July 1997. As it was, he told the editor of *The Daily Telegraph*, Charles Moore, two days before the handover, that all he had been able to do was to 'establish the agenda and to dominate it'. His advocates would argue that he should give himself more credit.

John Cole believes that in building a profile, or in attempting assessment of a politician, it is important to understand his self-image. 'Many of the most moving occasions of my life here have been inside a Church,' Patten told Charles Moore. He believes that the Christian faith in Asia is growing faster even than the economy. A Roman Catholic, Patten holds deep religious conviction, and he puts 'an interest in the human condition' high on his personal agenda.

His political philosophy thus has a strong moral and idealistic root. In the offices of the *South China Morning Post*, we were given a pile of Patten's speeches and articles published over the Hong Kong years, and in them, again and again, he circles around concepts of value, liberty and the human condition.

> On a hot, wet day in July [1992] I had been to a rehabilitation centre, and emerged to find a number of parents of handicapped children waiting in the rain to petition me. I was struck by their patience, by the moderation of their requests compared to the difficulties they faced, by their love and concern for their children. Those are qualities that I have met with time and time again here.

And again:

> Asia's growth has been driven by values but the values doing the driving are as British as they are Asian. They are ... universal. If I may paraphrase Theodore Roosevelt, the secret is to get yourself some good values and then get out of their way.

And finally:

> I have no doubt that in Asia as elsewhere the future is in the hands of those who can best combine political liberty and economic freedom.

Patten, in 1992, came to Hong Kong a convinced democrat and he was determined to strengthen Hong Kong's own democratic institutions as a safeguard against possible Chinese oppression after 1997. But here lies the rub, according to those dissatisfied with Patten. Himself a believer in the politics of pluralism, sometimes he did not seem to recognise the validity, or the necessity sometimes, of a different political imperative. To insist upon the universality of some values or upon the 'rightness' of one's way, should not debar one from recognising the sometime constraints of pace and context. It is this apparent inability to understand or make allowances for Beijing's difficulties in the management and ordering of its huge empire, whose problems were greatly exacerbated by the imminent prospect of the return to its bosom of a potentially difficult offspring – one which was quite out of step with the mainland and at a quite different stage in its maturing and political development – that demonstrated, for some, Patten's unsuitability as the Governor who was to preside over the transition of Hong Kong's sovereignty to China. The Chinese leadership had recently experienced a series of tremendous shocks and for them Hong Kong's imminent return to the Motherland would be good propaganda. But it was also a nightmare. Patten did not calm their fears; rather, he succeeded in frightening them out of their skins.

When Patten arrived as Governor in Hong Kong on 9 July 1992, certain agreements and arrangements had already been made between China

Familiar figure, Star Ferry, Kowloon. (Craig)

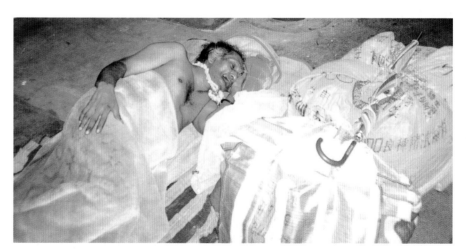

and Britain about the nature of the future Hong Kong constitution, and its laws and ways of life. We must bear this in mind in order to follow the cauldron of heated debate and mud-slinging which was to follow. In the ten years between 1982–92, from the beginning of Sino-British negotiations over the terms of the handover and the arrival of Chris Patten as Governor, Britain had found great difficulty in getting China to approve any increase in the democratic franchise for elections in Hong Kong; but it had been able, unattributably, to influence the drafting of the Basic Law which promised that, after 1997, Hong Kong would have an elected legislature, an accountable government and an independent judiciary. Chinese leaders would not interfere in Hong Kong affairs and its freedoms and way of life would continue for at least 50 years under the 'one country, two systems' policy. Britain also obtained a commitment from the Chinese that the last – 1995 elected – legislature under the British would be the first under the Chinese, the 'through train' concept. In the event, some of those who were elected (Martin Lee for one) had openly opposed Beijing's policies, and China would not contemplate a place for them.

A former ambassador to Beijing, Sir Robin McLaren, in a lecture at the Royal Institute of International Affairs, questioned whether the limited democratic improvements eventually won for the 1995 election to the Legislative Council and spearheaded by Patten justified the sacrifice of the 'through train' and the provoking of China into replacing the 1995 elected government at handover time with one unelected and appointed by Beijing. Sir Robin concluded that this must be 'a matter of judgement' and Patten has commented: 'I think that was a perfectly fair point; it is a matter of judgement'.

Patten himself believes that if he had not acted as he did, there would have been turbulence in Hong Kong, and demonstrations by Hong Kong Chinese who wanted democratic rights. He wrote in the *South China Morning Post* on 11 July 1996:

If we were to throw in our hand on this, what would we ever make a stand on? What then would be the basis for us blowing the whistle if things went wrong elsewhere, for example over the protection of Hong Kong's civil liberties?

Sir Percy Cradock, on the other side, argues in a *Daily Telegraph* article that Patten, in the end, harmed democracy in Hong Kong. 'By carrying through unilateral electoral change he ensured that Hong Kong passed under Chinese rule with less democracy than could have been the case.' Sir Percy believes, too, that any idea that there was a chance to promote democracy in the years before 1984 is unreal; the Chinese had made it plain that steps towards Westminster-style democracy would be totally unacceptable – and they had the power at any time to recover Hong Kong simply by cutting off the water and the food.

> Honour, or competence, in the Hong Kong context lay in securing the highest level of democracy that would endure after 1997, not in making short-term gestures which were bound to provoke a Chinese backlash and leave the colony worse off. No one condones Chinese actions. But they were entirely predictable, with repeated warnings. To go ahead with unilateral changes in these circumstances was, at best, a wild gamble with the future of 6.5 million people.

Of Patten's statement that in his electoral changes he was fulfilling a commitment in the Joint Declaration, Sir Percy has responded:

> Not so. Britain certainly had a political and moral obligation to secure for Hong Kong as much democracy as possible; but that meant democracy that would last beyond 1997, not a short self-serving show which we knew would only provoke a bad backlash ... It depends what you want. If you want to score points in some virility contest with China and be applauded in the press in Britain and America, all well and good. But if you are concerned with the protection of Hong Kong then we must recognise that no political institution will survive time unless it is underwritten by China.

Sir Percy's point about 'a wild gamble with the future of 6.5 million people' is a crucial one, for in making judgements about past courses of action, one cannot fairly use knowledge gained from benefit of hindsight. When he adopted his electoral reform plan Patten faced a future untold: what, at that time, was the balance of risk?

Hong Kong is the only colony which was not left with self-rule when the British hung up their boots. For all that, Hong Kong was a prosperous society enjoying the fruits of democracy, apart from the lack of a fully democratic electoral system. Its citizens enjoyed the rule of law, an independent judiciary and freedom of speech. Other former colonies left by the British with full independence and self-rule were not so ordered, free or prosperous as Hong Kong. The point here is a simple one: Hong Kong was odd, a one-off, even unique. Run by an administration with a competent, uncorrupt civil service and its liberties underpinned by the Parliament at Westminster, it was an enormously successful society, even if headed by a patriarchal British Governor.

Four events, occurring before Patten's arrival, were to have a significant impact upon Hong Kong, and the shape of its future as defined in the Joint Sino-British Declaration and in the Basic Law. The first was the Falklands War in 1982. The British Prime Minister, having retained British sovereignty over the Falkland Islands, having kept them

HMY Britannia docks near Prince of Wales Barracks with the Convention Centre in the background. (Craig)

intact from the marauding intentions of Argentina, triumphant, next became determined to keep Hong Kong after 1997 (when the lease would run out for the New Territories). This was impractical, and she came to acknowledge that all Hong Kong must return to China in July 1997. However, the whole issue of Hong Kong moved to centre stage.

The second significant event was the Tiananmen Square massacre in Beijing in 1989 and the shocked response of the world. Particularly relevant in this context was the shocked response in Hong Kong, where one million people took to the streets in protest. Fears of repression after 1997, and intolerance of demonstrations which had become a way of life in Hong Kong, accelerated thoughts towards the broadening of the electoral system. In turn, the Beijing leadership reacted with horror to the troublesome protests in Hong Kong, particularly in regard to the effect such behaviour might have upon latent dissidence on the south China coast, whose inhabitants enjoyed watching Hong Kong television. This situation was exacerbated by television activity itself. According to the Royal Hong Kong Police 150th Anniversary report;

> In reaction to the Tiananmen Square incident of 1989, criminals tried to shroud looting with patriotism. The trouble was extinguished within minutes [this refers to the work of the Hong Kong Police Tactical Unit] although global television which replayed endlessly one 30-second segment made it seem Hong Kong was in flames. In reality PTUs had quenched the riot before it began.

Thus Tiananmen Square fed mutual fear between Beijing and Hong Kong; Hong Kong was to think more of freedom, Beijing of control.

After 4 June 1989, Hong Kong's Governor had two main options. Under the first he could try to keep China calm; effect a smooth transition; see the arrival of the 'through train' and, on 1 July, see Hong Kong retain its partially elected Legislative Council. This option, many believed, would chime with China's now well-established progress in the development of a free market, which had been instituted by Deng Xiaoping and which had brought increased trading ties between China and Hong Kong; but there was at the same time no realistic hope for the demise of the communist form of political rule in the near future, hence Deng Xiaoping's formula 'one country, two systems' – the recognition of this political fact. The second option was for Hong Kong to go for further democratisation, winning China's approval, if possible.

The first approach was favoured by those who believed that the Sino-British agreement had gone as far as China would agree and that in any case no arrangement not approved by China would last after 1997. The second had support within Hong Kong from those who had already tried for a broadening of the democratic franchise, which had taken form in the 1991 elections. Martin Lee was involved in these earlier moves and the Tiananmen Square massacre had turned him into a hero, as the population's thoughts were brutally concentrated on politics. And, of course, the democrats found in the massacre propaganda for their cause.

The third impinging event was the British General Election in April 1992. The Conservatives were re-elected to govern, partly as a result of the industry of the Party Chairman, Chris Patten, but at that election, Patten himself lost his seat as member of Parliament for the Bath constituency.

The fourth major factor was Prime Minister John Major's visit to China in 1992 which Beijing had made a prerequisite of its (necessary) approval of the construction of a new airport for Hong Kong. The Chinese government was nervous of the airport project, which it believed would eat up the Hong Kong billion-dollar reserve – to be part of its prize in 1997. John Major, some said, felt he had suffered humiliation in Beijing. After the General Election he appointed his friend, the architect of the Conservative Party electoral victory, to be the new Governor of Hong Kong, which spelt the departure of the then Governor, Sir David Wilson, who would have backed the 'through train'.

So far as Patten is concerned, on his arrival in Hong Kong in July 1992, the tide of democracy was already rising and he claims, quite reasonably, that he was not the initiator of this current in Hong Kong affairs, and that his contribution had been to encourage and facilitate democratisation, to the extent that he was able within the parameters of the 1984 Declaration. In his own words, he tried to find 'elbow-room' within this framework to extend the electoral element in the constitution of the Legislative Council believing that he could 'get away with it'. But in so doing – for his projected bill eventually did become law – he so raised the stakes with the Chinese government that he brought upon his own head a rain of vituperation and a permanent alienation from the Chinese leaders.

Patten did not think he should play by China's rules. The leaders of Beijing were bullies and for him to have appeased them so as to keep them talking, would have been to make unacceptable concessions. Critics of Patten say that he was like a bull in a china shop just at the time when what was needed was a dealer in fine porcelain. Above all China needed reassurance, for Tiananmen had raised ghosts of the Red Guards.

When we returned to England, people asked us about Jonathan Dimbleby's book *The Last Governor*, and we watched a video of his five-part BBC television series. In Hong Kong, we had been surprised to learn of the book's early publication; could the account of the Governor's years, his performance in such a tricky situation, written so soon, be helpful, reliable? An interesting read, perhaps, but we wondered whether any professional historian would have even contemplated the idea. The passage of time has brought forth truth, or a reasonable version of events, out of many an early muddle. And how wise was it, further, for Patten to permit the entry into Government House of this old school friend, this television man, accompanied by cameras, which were to record comments about top level conversations relating to Hong Kong's future and highly sensitive negotiations with the Chinese?

To many, Patten in these programmes did not appear judicious; indeed that acumen, clarity, quickness of mind manifest in his own writings, seemed absent. Instead, he seemed self-satisfied, blunt, arrogant. But the camera can lie, indeed is potentially explosive, even self-destructive. The wise are always wary of it. The most misleading aspect of these programmes was their failure to present to any useful degree, if at all, the problem China is to itself, and the problems Hong Kong presented to the Beijing leadership. In the programmes, Chinese negotiators, representatives, leaders, came over as in a soap opera, like cardboard men or, as in a bad Western, with Patten the goody in the white hat, in a shoot-out with the baddies – the cowboy hero from the West contemplating the rough, untamed East.

The book itself, published so soon after Patten's departure from Hong Kong and apparently containing some dramatic revelations, caused a stir: good for circulation and audience ratings but was it good for Hong Kong and for Sino-British relations at this delicate but tremendously important time in Hong Kong's history? Again, it is a matter of judgement.

John Major, who, under Margaret Thatcher, had held the post of Foreign Secretary for nine weeks only, was contemptuous of some aspects of diplomacy when he appointed Chris Patten to Hong Kong. It is not surprising, therefore, that from the time of Patten's appointment, a new way was adopted of conducting affairs relating to Hong Kong. Under Major, from 1992, Beijing and the British Foreign Office were deliberately sidelined.

Governor Patten told *Asiaweek*, on 20 October 1993, that his only concern 'is to do what is in Hong Kong's best interest'. The magazine was not convinced:

> From the start, Mr Patten's approach all but ensured that the cause would be lost. By abruptly going it alone with his constitutional proposals, he fed Beijing's worst fears about British sincerity on consultation and co-operation. His abrasive, grandstanding manner and his skilful manipulation of media to portray the tussle as a struggle between good and evil, at times seemed almost calculated to draw the most belligerent response possible from Chinese officials, who can be as nasty as anyone.

Asiaweek threw further light on Governor Patten's possible motivations. Widely tipped as a future Prime Minister, at least by the 'fawning English-language media', he 'would put his own political future uppermost ... his credentials will be immeasurably strengthened if he is seen, at home, to have performed a tough job in Hong Kong honourably in defence of British values'. As the inhabitants of Bath might say: 'It's a matter of judgement.'

The Governor's final speech at the Farewell Parade. (Craig)

CHAPTER 24

30 JUNE – THE PARADE

Pat McLinden, Drum Major 1st Bn. The Black Watch (RHR) sat at a desk in the Pipes and Drums office at Redford Barracks, Edinburgh, looking at a photograph of himself with an amused smile.

> The rain was horrendous … Our uniforms were being destroyed. I remember thinking … Christ! my uniform is going to be wrecked and I need it for the Edinburgh Tattoo straight away.

His eyes sparkled – he had just been interviewed about the impending Pipes and Drums North American tour – and memories were flooding back.

> I remember thinking … spats … white coming off … hackles ruined … nothing quite like it before. Even my gloves were hanging off, they were so heavy with moisture … but my grip on the Mace was all right! … we knew we had a huge television audience … We knew there was no turning back. We did it for the Black Watch … stretched ourselves up … had to do the parade properly … took my lead from the Scots Guards Drum Major … could see him.

He went quiet, for a moment, at the recollection. 'Yes … it was noticeable … a bigger cheer when we came on … there's a big Scottish contingent in Hong Kong.' Normally, he said, you could see people's expressions, as for instance, at the Edinburgh Tattoo, but you were not close enough in Hong Kong. You could not see what emotions were being felt, so did not hear the usual feedback from the audience, which is always such a help. So the cheers were wonderful. 'If only we could have had 24 hours after the parade to enjoy the atmosphere – it would have been nice to have had a couple of days to enjoy Hong Kong.' He was still a wee bit disappointed, too, about the rain; the audience would have had a bigger spectacle in the sun but he had to admit the rain had added spice: 'Funny thing, every time Prince Charles mentioned the Queen, it seemed to rain harder!'

As we cross to Stonecutters' Island by the military launch on the morning of 30 June 1997 we are both silently reviewing the events of the past couple of months, wondering what the day will bring and how the next weeks will unfold without the Hong Kong garrison, for over 150 years such a part of the city's fabric and daily ritual. In much the same way, the next day, 1 July , will demonstrate that one of the unsung bulwarks of this magical city has gone.

Nonetheless we step onto Stonecutters' for the last time with keen

Final early morning clear-up at Stonecutters' Island, 30 June 1997. (Craig)

anticipation and make our way past the silent shipyards – it is a public holiday – to the first sentry box. The sky looks distinctly ominous and we both have the feeling that rain is inevitable. We have also been told that the parade will be cancelled if it pours.

Morning has begun for the Black Watch at 0100 hrs when the last container goes to LSL. I recall early reveille at my final training camp, Trawsfynydd, in North Wales. At some ungodly hour, as we all sleep the sleep of the just, after strenuous exercises in the surrounding hills, an NCO seizes an iron bar and trails it along the corrugated iron wall of our hut at head height. 'Wakey! Wakey! ... Even the dead must rise.'

Here in Hong Kong, at 0630 hrs, the Royal Navy Guard (from HMS *Illustrious*) disembark from RFA *Sir Percivale* and move to the NAAFI. With breakfast at 0700 hrs, groups are quartering the island picking up non-existent litter, and by 0900 hrs the last three vehicles have left taking television sets and weighing machines to 'Disposals'. At the Prince of Wales Barracks 'the whole day was hectic. Lots of panic and flap from upstairs – every five minutes the situation would change ... Colonels were in and out changing plans every five minutes.' The Black Watch Officer responsible for PR and the battalion photographer both lose their accreditation. Security is tightening.

On Hong Kong Island the Chief Executive Designate, Tung Chee Hwa, has been working at his office in the Asia Pacific Finance Tower since before 0800 hrs. At 1000 hrs Carabiner International – the company producing the Farewell Parade – announces to Major General Bryan Dutton, Commander British Forces, that the show is overrunning by 15 minutes. Please cut.

Stonecutters': all personnel are now clear of their accommodation, which has also been cleaned. Holding areas: NAAFI, Cookhouse, D Block Hall, Sergeants' Mess and Officers' Mess. All operational ammunition and remaining blank ammo has been moved by truck to HMS *Chatham*.

A bus driver wraps up a television set with tender care in a large sheet and staggers with it to his bus. Emerging breathless, he gives a bow and a smile. Around are groups of cleaning ladies and tea ladies picking through skips and chattering together, saying goodbyes or having little 'parties'. From midnight they will have no jobs and what future?

There is no coffee in the Officers' Mess, just a pile of tinned drinks. We pass lovely tropical green shrubs and palms, with sporadic yellow, orange and red roses, other yellow blooms and a cactus-type shrub below the Quartermaster's window.

Meet the HQ Coy. tea-lady who had had her farewell presentation three days earlier; take her address and promise to send copies of the photographs that had been taken. Ask if there is any chance of tea – it is very hot. She shoots away to return with steaming mugs on a tray, which she presents with full Chinese charm, and chats as we drink. 'Goodbye,' she says at the end. 'You come back to Hong Kong.' Her eyes brim. 'You come back.'

Meanwhile, the Royal Gurkha Rifles Pipes and Drums and the Royal Marine Band (HMS *Illustrious*) and the Royal Naval Guard (HMS *Illustrious*) muster on Stonecutters' Square. A message reaches Lieutenant Colonel Price, Director of Music Scots Guards and Senior Director of Music Guards Division, to telephone Major General Dutton without delay. But – no telephones. The only telephones remaining are in the hands of the People's Liberation Army. But this is Hong Kong. Colonel Price approaches the nearest group of tea ladies. 'Anyone got a mobile phone I could use?' (All Hong Kong local calls are free.) One appears in a flash, amidst giggles. 'But don't call Blittain ... Don't call Blittain.'

Colonel Price gets in touch with General Dutton's Executive Officer who tells him to 'get over here – quick'. Right, but there is a reduced ferry service so he has to go through the tunnel. Get a car. No cars. All military cars already at 'Disposals'. Quick search uncovers two 'sold' cars awaiting shipment. Colonel Price commandeers one and heads for Prince of Wales Barracks.

He arrives at a tense meeting, to hear the whole programme has to be cut by 15 minutes, the military to take six minutes out. Is asked for his opinion. 'No.' He says firmly that they had warned Carabiner on the two previous nights that they were 15 minutes adrift. 'Oh, that's fine,' they had said. 'We'll deal with it, etc etc' Then, on the last day, the penny drops: 'Can you cut 15 minutes?' No!

General Dutton, who had previously stated on television how very proud he was of the contribution the British garrison had made to Hong Kong ('made it an oasis of stability in a part of the world where this was not everywhere so') and of the relationship between the garrison and the people of Hong Kong, makes his decision.

> If Her Majesty made that request I'd do it. If the Governor made that request I'd argue with all my power but would probably do it in the end. But if anyone else asks me … the answer is absolutely not!

At RAF Uxbridge, months later, he told us, with a disarming smile:

> No … I won't tell you what I actually said to them. Well … you see there was no possible time for a rehearsal, even an abbreviated one … Yes … they asked me at 1000 hrs in the morning just when I was right in the middle of many other things, phone calls … the last day was very hectic.

What the Pipes and Drums, Bands and Guards thought was pungent. 'An amateur outfit' and 'nae foresight' are two of the rare printable offerings.

We walk around Stonecutters', pausing to examine skips which are collected hourly from 1100 hrs, and watch the Queen's Colour Squadron, RAF Regiment, at some final rehearsal. This is worth seeing. The Guard is being put through its paces by F/Sgt Bennett who causes further tremors of recognition from National Service days. Always immaculate, he is a mobile Ben Nevis with perfection his aim. A run-through is drawing to its finish and I am impressed; not so F/Sgt Bennett. 'What's the matter with you lot?' he roars. 'You've disconnected your bloody brains … pull your socks up or we'll be here all day.' His Guard take it all stoically. After another try, as they march back to start all over again, a corporal murmurs to the airman next to him: 'Don't think of it as a job, son; look on it as an enriching experience.'

One of the many minor problems to be overcome *vis-à-vis* the Parade was the question of pace. Highlanders march to the swing of the kilt, the Navy are slow and roll along (they have no reason to be quick) and the RAF are fast (116–120 paces to the minute) 'to make themselves look good. They do a shorter pace – 26 ins instead of 30 ins – to make it possible'. A compromise had to be agreed upon.

The RAF did not want to come into line with the Black Watch and the Navy and in the heat and tension ancient inter-service rivalries rear their heads. The Navy? 'Thinks it's superior and that's all the thinking it does.' The RAF? 'A load of bastards, who will do anything to show up others.' The Black Watch? 'Just a bunch of big-arsed swaggerers.' It all depends on your Service viewpoint. Naturally, when the moment comes, the Black Watch surpass themselves, the Queen's Colour Squadron are near perfection and the Navy are generally agreed, through sheer hard work, to be on a par with their junior partners. Indeed some say they were best, adding though, that such distinctions are invidious in view of the united impact.

The RAF Regiment are the only ones who, nowadays, are taught how to slow march – essential for the final *Auld Lang Syne* exit. But the Navy said the RAF were not going to teach them how to do it; and the Black Watch said we won't be told by the RAF either so ... until Colonel Loudon said get on with it and then they all co-operated. The temperature is 33.5°C and the humidity at record levels.

Meanwhile, at Stonecutters' the Queen's Colour Squadron, their brains re-connected, are having an early lunch before mustering to take the 1200 hrs ferry to Prince of Wales Barracks, and we see the Quartermaster briefly.

'The PLA were in here this morning. I had to chase them out.'
'Keen?'
'Aye – too keen.'

Leaving him to his final handover to the Government Land Agency, we head for what we hope will be a ferry in 15 minutes' time, passing, *en*

The Drum Major has doubts about the weather, 1pm. Military Ferry 30 June 1997.

(Craig)

route, the Medical Officer and his sergeant who are in good heart with no casualties and no one sick; and Colonel Loudon, who says 'hello' quietly and then walks on up the hill to his house – a lone figure in shorts with a can of Coke.

When we reach the embarkation jetty it seems unusually quiet and two Chinese seamen tell us that the next ferry is at 1300 hrs. So we sit around, write notes and absorb the sudden stillness where there is usually the noisy bustling of boats. The new masters will soon break the silence. Suddenly we realise there is no activity on board our ferry. We leg it to where we can see the Black Watch Pipes and Drums, the Highland Band and the Black Watch Guard boarding their launch for the Prince of Wales Barracks.

The Guard Commander, Major Cole-Mackintosh, is full of optimism that the weather will stay fair and says so. Drum Major McLinden disagrees and says so more pungently. Otherwise the atmosphere here is quiet as well. They have been up since around 0600 hrs, have rehearsed yet again, finished all the innumerable jobs moving out entails and are dressed in full fig. It is very hot and they must wait until 1700 hrs before they start mustering for the parade.

We land at POWB pier. The Pipes and Drums are none too pleased at being kept hanging about in front of their own barracks. Security is tightening. At the NAAFI by the swimming pool, with last snacks and mugs of refreshing tea, final farewells are going on all around. Staff gather in ever-changing groups exchanging gifts and talking, because for all of them it really is the end of an era. Years and years of devoted service to the British garrison will end this midnight.

While we eat and gaze the Army's meticulous planning swings into action:

1300–1330 QCS use lifts in POWB to get to WDS and Sgts Mess.

22nd Floor

1345–1355 1BW P&D use lifts in POWB to move to Offrs Mess.

26th Floor

1355–1410 Hld Band use lifts in POWB to move to Offrs Mess.

26th Floor

1400 Tri-Sve Handover Gd departs SCI on Ferry for HK CEC
1410–1440 1BW Gd use lifts in POWB to move to Offrs Mess.

26th Floor

The Pipes and Drums are delayed by tightening security at the Prince of Wales Barracks. 30 June 1997.

(Craig)

In Central, at the Mandarin Oriental Hotel, where Michelle Abbott, the American harpist, often plays, the foyer and lounge are, of course, bursting with activity – those one wants to see and those who want to be seen – but the usual serene Mandarin ambience is still in evidence. Nothing could ever jolt the staff here out of their impeccable stride. At the City Hall Low Block there is definitely something in the air, though what exactly is hard to tell. Though the Parade tickets say arrive at 1600 hrs, crowds are already edging forwards.

At the Convention Centre, the Tri-Service Handover Guard has settled behind the partitions screening them from the main hall. The PLA are in their changing room. There is plenty of space for all. They do some final rehearsals, check timings just to make sure. Earlier rehearsals have gone well because 'there was no interference ... the brass could not get in ... no problems at all with the indoor ceremony'.

'The first rehearsal with the PLA was nerve-racking,' says a Jock. 'They were like robots, didn't do anything unless told to by an officer.' But everything soon calms down, the Garrison Sergeant Major gets on well with his counterpart and they all become acclimatised to the bright lights and the various timings, which have to be exact for the flags.

The PLA uniforms are all new. The British forces regard the naval one as 'quite funny with its ribbons at the back'. But the PLA impress everyone with their drill. Are their rifles wooden or real? (They are real.) They have a special team ready for *the* big night.

Back on Stonecutters' the very last skip is being collected. As of 1600 hrs the island is clear.

The queues at the City Hall Low Block are getting longer but moving steadily through the various bag searches, x-rays and metal detector archways. The police are there in force and the crowds good-humoured. It has started to drizzle and people smile at one another. Just how bad will it get? Everyone collects a programme and a complimentary blue and yellow umbrella.

The Governor is leaving Government House for the last time and omitting to circle the driveway three times as insurance for a return visit some day. The Adjutant 1BW finds he has four crates of lemonade and five of Coke left when he has finished sorting out the bar. Seeing Chinese staff with a car outside, he asks: 'Do you want these?' Vigorous nods, crates heaved into boot and a very low-slung car heads slowly for Kowloon. The Adjutant says:

O.P. at the border. Crest
Hill. June 1997.

(Frank Proctor)

Nothing has to be left, even the drawing pins in the drawing boards. Piles of paper. All to be cleared. Anything left would belong to the Hong Kong government. *Nothing* must be left to inconvenience the People's Liberation Army.

1715 hrs: President Jiang Zemin and Premier Li Peng arrive at Kai Tak airport with Mrs Deng Xiaoping and daughter. They are met by Rita Fan. At Stonecutters', the PLA and the Government Property Agency turn up. Final handover completed; flag down, out of Guardroom; gates closed.

All 1BW Support Troops depart on Ferry 'EE' at 1800 hrs for Kowloon Point on the way to Kai Tak airport. It is a small vessel and the water unexpectedly choppy so that the Black Watch Accounts Officer has a nightmare vision of the battalions' accounts being swept over the heaving stern.

1915–1945	1BW Sci Sp Tps change into civilian clothes
1955	1BW Sci Sp Tps arrive at Departure Lounge

In the Arena the arriving guests are serenaded by the Massed Bands of the Royal Hong Kong Police and the Royal Hong Kong Auxiliary Police. They pipe and drum and dance with the very best and the rain begins to fall. Soon there is a sea of umbrellas – the complimentary ones proving just the right size to protect while avoiding neighbourly clashes. The atmosphere is friendly, good-natured, with appropriate remarks when a Hong Kong Club umbrella – naturally twice as large as any other – proves difficult to accommodate without someone getting a steady cascade down front or back.

1815: The Farewell Ceremony begins with a youthful Dragon Dance. What else? Hong Kong is a Chinese city. The Dragon symbolises energy, vitality, purity, intelligence, wisdom and good luck. Hong Kong possesses the first five in abundance; the packed audience hope it will have much of the sixth in the years ahead.

1820: Prince Charles leaves *Britannia* for the Arena to a 21-gun salute. From where we sit we can see the official car leaving the quayside, confirm it on the two giant TV screens or watch the colourful gyrations of the exuberant Dragons as the 21 explosive crumps crack off the surrounding skyscrapers. Hong Kong harbour is alive. Beyond HMS *Chatham* are pleasure-craft, police launches, rigid inflatables, all with flashing lights plus the usual ferryings – a vibrant kaleidoscope of movement. A Royal Fanfare and the programme proper begins.

At nearby Prince of Wales Barracks the 1BW Guard is moving from the 26th to the ground floor – in groups of 24 (six per lift). The Black Watch and Royal Gurkha Rifles Pipes and Drums are both already there – the adrenalin beginning to flow. Would the rain get worse? Yes, is the general pithily expressed opinion. Would they cancel? No! Only a typhoon would stop them now! The Navy and the RAF agree.

In the Arena, the rain eases off a bit, as a crowd of hundreds represents the Spirit of Hong Kong, dressed as everything from a junk to a mobile phone with, of course, someone as the essential golden dollar; an evocation of Hong Kong's people, its culture and emergence as a powerful modern economic dragon, all to music from the Hong Kong (Traditional) Chinese Orchestra founded in 1977 and winning a high reputation abroad, and the equally renowned (Classical) Hong Kong Philharmonic Orchestra.

Actor Brian Blessed and singer Frances Yip continue the programme as the rain begins to fall again, descending to the dais with firmly clutched umbrellas. As an actor and the oldest man to climb to 28,000 feet without oxygen, and an international Chinese star with 80 albums in more than a dozen languages to her credit, these two are unlikely to be fazed by a shower. The evening is beginning to take on a spirit of its own and the crowd to coalesce. As it is difficult to juggle umbrella, programme and camera, a united decision has been reached, by some kind of collective osmosis, that the crowd will applaud by stamping its feet on the aluminium stands – which makes a gratifying noise.

Back in POWB, the Bands, the Pipes and Drums and the Guards chat, put finishing touches to uniforms and watch the rain.

Next come Hong Kong's 'little good-will singing ambassadors', the Hong Kong Children's Choir who, for many people, underline the kind of future they are all striving for. Watching them sing their hearts out in

Young Hong Kong residents rehearse for the Farewell Parade.

(Craig)

the pouring rain – especially on television close-ups – brings many a moist eye. The rain seems to be getting harder. The orchestras play under opened umbrellas – a rare and entertaining sight.

At Stonecutters', the PLA are sussing out their new domain and finding it 'immaculate', as some of them told me weeks later, laying cables and checking to see what sort of bugging devices might have been left by their departing hosts. They find the set-up to their liking.

The Ceremony moves on, with vocal performances and musical interludes, to the Governor's address, a chance to sum it all up. Hong Kong would now run itself: 'That is the promise and that is the unshakeable destiny.' The stands take a hammering.

Now the military take over: the Massed Bands of the Royal Marines, the Scots Guards and the Scottish Division (The Highland Band) with the Pipes and Drums of the 1st Battalion the Black Watch and the Brigade of Gurkhas. 'Quite a tricky task,' said Lieutenant Colonel Price, Director of Music to the Guards Division, afterwards. 'Unusual, with three military bands and two pipe bands and little rehearsal time ... keeping contact with them all was a problem ... The Scots Guards, for instance, were Trooping the Colour in London and then flew out on the Sunday

The Hong Kong Philharmonic Orchestra plays in the rain. (Craig)

afterwards. Then later on the Marine Bands came from *Illustrious* and *Britannia*. They were not all together until the last week ... And no ... there was no chance of getting a PLA Band into the Farewell Parade. Politically, it could not have happened.'

They swing into their routine and the Arena buzzes with anticipation. And then the Pipes and Drums – Black Watch and Gurkhas intermingled – burst into view and there is tumultuous applause and the grandstands take even more hammering. The rain is getting heavier and the crowd, one unified body now, are all getting wet but there is a distinct feeling of 'what the hell' in the air.

Finally, after their long wait, come the Guards of Honour – Royal Navy, Black Watch and Royal Air Force. The Navy, sailors from HMS *Illustrious* and HMS *Chatham*, come on in great style and are duly cheered; and then the Pipes and Drums play *Hielan' Laddie* for the Black Watch and a growl comes from the crowd that grows into a thunderous roar and stamping of feet. 'Christ! These stands are taking one hell of a battering,' says someone. 'And they haven't been tested yet,' answers an unperturbed voice.

'When we appeared ... tremendous applause ... gave us a terrific lift – just to hear that ... put us on a high,' said the Black Watch RSM, Alan

McEwan, months later in Fort George, Inverness. 'We were centre stage ... the public got our spirits up – it was the best thing we could have hoped for.'

And so, through the Royal Salute and the National Anthem to the Royal Address. Prince Charles steps forward. And then the heavens open. Torrential, drenching downpour. The crowd knows he must be soaked but it is only on the TV screens that one can see the water building up behind the gold braid of his cap and cascading past his face.

Officially the Prince is to speak for two minutes and he must realise that many, for one reason or another, hope he cuts it short. No doubt he himself would like to do so. However, most also realise that he is HM The Queen's messenger to Hong Kong, and as such has no option but to deliver Her speech as written. It seems a very long two minutes. 'Every time Prince Charles mentioned the Queen, it seemed to rain harder!' The crowd's reaction is at first one of collective distress – a general feeling that enough is enough and that this last lashing torrent is going too far. But, at the same time, that very harshness moves the crowd to a higher level of participation. One naval officer says, 'If they can do it so can I' and folds up his umbrella; two brother officers follow suit. A member of the Hong Kong Club steps into the open and stands there, utterly drenched, with an expression of great pride on his face, muttering support to the troops. Some reactions:

'We knew we were being appreciated.'
'When the heavens opened ... that was it, that was the moment.'
'We were determined not to let the rain make it awful.'

One of the Colour Bearers said, 'It was really heavy ... and the ground was very wet ... holding the colours horizontally.' During the dress rehearsal, he had had a muscle cramp in his right arm and was praying this would not happen today of all days. This is the first time out for the genuine Colours. The practice flags are lighter, but the real ones are better balanced; nevertheless, torrential rain increases their weight well beyond any expectations and makes for a very long two minutes. 'I was so relieved to hoist them back.' Moments after leaving the Arena, the Colours are covered again, to be boxed later at Kai Tak.

The troops stand grimly to dripping attention and must wonder, as do the crowd, if their ordeal will ever end. Their white jackets, specially made in Shenzen, are being ruined; their hackles run red dye. The Scots Guards Band will be playing in the Convention Centre shortly after this parade. Mercifully, they have different uniforms for that Ceremony but what on earth will their bearskins look like – even their medal-ribbon colours are running into each other? The sheer noise of the downpour is stunning.

It is over. Prince Charles returns to his seat, remarking to General Dutton later, 'that was the best speech I ever made under water', and the Ceremony moves on to Sunset and the lowering of the Union and Hong Kong flags. When the Lone Piper – Pipe Major Stephen Small – marches forward the rain reaches a crescendo. There is so much water it may drown the reeds. His lone figure playing *The Immortal Memory* seems to epitomise regimental pipers down the ages.

Now, a *Feu de Joie* and the Guards of Honour march off – slow march – *to Auld Lang Syne*. During all the rehearsals of these steps, no one dreamt they would be put to such a vigorous test. The stands again take a battering but there is much less shouting – most people are struggling to cope with the lumps in their throats.

Now the Finale: the Massed Bands, Pipes and Drums, Orchestras, Choirs and Cast with the theme song for the handover – *Rhythm of My Heart*.

Why tears? What is Hong Kong to us or us to Hong Kong that we should weep for her, we wonder, emotions mangling the Bard? It is the young Chinese, faces aglow with pride and expectation – 'What can be imagined can be achieved' – and singing with full-throated joy that hit the heart. *They* are 'the promise' and *they* are 'the unshakeable destiny'.

CHAPTER 25

30 JUNE – CONVENTION CENTRE

As matters turned out, the Scots Guards Band had a 90-minute gap before they had to perform at the Convention Centre and, finding a hair-dryer from somewhere, managed to dry their bearskins and medals and look immaculate when they next appeared on stage. This Band, first formed by King Charles I, were representing Britain at this ceremony because they wear bearskins and it was thought that these would be appropriate to the occasion.

Today's Band number 49, picked from the finest instrumentalists to be found in the Services. They are stationed in London and are present at various state occasions in the UK. They have toured the USA, Canada, Kenya, Germany, Italy, France, Spain, Malta, Cyprus, Australia and Hong Kong.

For the warm-up, the Chinese Band played three pieces of music and then the Scots Guards played three of their choice. The musicians felt that they were less formal than the various tri-service guards – there were no barriers and the Chinese were 'great musicians ... great fun to work with ... great jam sessions!' All the musicians 'got stuck in, swapped CDs, swapped plaques'. They shared an art which they both appreciated ... they respected each other.

The 4,000 guests at the Convention Centre had chilled champagne, which may not have been quite as refreshing as normal as they shivered damply in the air-conditioning. From there, they moved into a banqueting hall approximately the size of four football pitches. As the dignitaries and guests ate smoked salmon and chicken, the first detachment of the People's Liberation Army crossed the border into the New Territories. Still damp, everyone moved to yet another hall for the official Handover Ceremony; it was here that the Band of the Scots Guards and the tri-service Guards were waiting to perform. It was, on the whole, surprising that the Centre was, though 'not totally complete' and still missing a few roof tiles, ready for use. A target date of 23 June had actually been set for completion of the roof, but heavy rain had wreaked havoc with the schedule. However, the managing director of the Centre said the tiles were purely aesthetic and there was no chance of leaks. Water did, however, drop onto various guests throughout the proceedings.

Prince Charles talked to the Tri-Service Guards and so did General Dutton which was much appreciated. Photographs were taken, pleasantries exchanged and last minute adjustments were made. The Garrison Sergeant Major, Vince Bell, had been asked several times all about his Pace-Stick, so he presented one to his opposite number to that gentleman's great delight.

At 2330 hrs the ceremony starts. British and Chinese leaders sit on a stage specially built in the Grand Hall, with a spectacular view over Victoria Harbour. At 2350 hrs, Prince Charles gives his farewell speech. At a few minutes before midnight, the Union flag and the Hong Kong flag are lowered as the Scots Guards play the National Anthem.

'On the night I was behind the flag-pole, just waiting for something to happen, but it didn't ... we had to adjust to the PLA's movements ... speed up to match them, then slow down ... compensate.'

A member of the Black Watch Guard.

They had thought very carefully about the flags and how to make things look right. National flags hanging limp on a night like this would be unacceptable, so they devised a system whereby a man underneath the stage controlled an air-cylinder which sent a stream of air up the poles and out of a single vent a third of the way up the flags. The cylinder operator knew from practice how much pressure to apply to get just the right breeze. And to make doubly sure they attached a fishing line to both top and bottom shackles of the flags and fastened it to the edging with Velcro, so that the man below stage could apply pressure and keep the flag taut. He knew from markers whereabouts it was on its journey down the pole. This meant, of course, that the Guards unhitching the flags, when they had been lowered, not only had to deal with the normal shackles but also had to make sure that the fishing line was untied and unzipped from the Velcro so that it could be swiftly whipped out of sight – all with unhurried dignity. They practised it a lot.

Members of the PLA Guard and Band watch President Jiang Zemin arriving at the Convention Centre. 30 June 1997. (Vince Bell)

Just after midnight the Chinese and SAR flags are raised and the Chinese President Jiang Zemin, the first People's Republic of China Head of State to visit Hong Kong, addresses the audience. Ten minutes later, the ceremony draws to a close and Prince Charles and ex-Governor Patten take their leave.

Colonel David Price, Director of Music, told us: 'After the ceremony … that's when we felt it … quite sad really … the boys felt it, yes.' He was appointed Director of Music to Her Majesty's Scots Guards in 1987 and in 1993 became Senior Director of Music Guards Division, responsible for co-ordinating all the music played at various State occasions such as The Queen's Birthday Parade, Beating Retreat, the Festival of Remembrance and the Cenotaph Parade.

At 0130 hrs, the Scots Guards Band, 1BW and QCS Handover Gd. Pers. hand in instruments, change into civilian clothes and make their way to the Departure Lounge at the airport.

Organising final details at Kai Tak airport.

(JSPRS)

CHAPTER 26

30 JUNE –
PRINCE OF WALES BARRACKS

M idnight. The Prince of Wales Barracks. It took, literally, seconds. Lieutenant Colonel Jeremy Ellis, of the Queen's Gurkha Signals, was in charge. He handed over to a People's Liberation Army Colonel. The Black Watch positioned two sentries. The People's Liberation Army positioned two sentries. The Gurkha Colonel took a pace forward. The People's Liberation Army Colonel took a pace forward. The Gurkha Colonel wished them good luck and they shook hands. It was done.

Black Watch versus the People's Liberation Army, Carlsberg International 10s, Hong Kong. (JSPRS)

Black Watch, Red Dawn. *(Frank Proctor)*

The previous few hours had been fraught. The PLA had made heavy demands, outside earlier agreements, which would never have been entertained five days earlier.

The garrison hierarchy had gone, however, and it was agreed that argument, at this stage, would be indulgent. But for a while there was a real feeling of control slipping away and there was confusion and anger. 'These are *our* barracks until midnight.'

The PLA were the new masters and so they arrived half an hour early. They were trying to hustle the takeover. Jumping from their lorries, they erected a large Countdown Clock. They were all at least 6' 2" and had been specially chosen and trained for this one night. The press – including their own – were with them in force and flash bulbs were exploding all the time.

We could find no empathy with these PLA troops, as we had with the Advance Guard; these were faceless. The barracks were immaculate, we were ready to welcome them and they ... we were ready to mix it, you know.

Then, after discussion, agreement was reached about the brief Handover Ceremony and the garrison felt they had taken back some initiative.

Chinese staff who had worked with the garrison for up to 25 years were standing watching – the emotion on their faces plain to see. Those not involved with the Guard left the barracks and moved across the roadway, in groups, to stand on the quayside by HMS *Chatham*. 'We were sad ... we did feel we were leaving with our tails between our legs.'

Finally, just before midnight, the strains of the National Anthem floated towards them and the Union Jack was lowered. Then, as the stroke of the hour sounded, the Chinese flag was raised and the Chinese National Anthem was heard across the parade ground. The Guard marched, through the cheering crowd to the ferry for Kai Tak Airport, where the rest joined them. 'They formed up ... then marched out ... looking dignified.' Everyone else went on board, the Jocks waved and the crowd sang. 'I was never prouder to wear the hackle.'

RED DAWN

One morning a couple of weeks after reunification I walked along the brand new roadway to Prince of Wales Barracks, bowed to the rather severe-looking sentry and asked if I could see someone who spoke English, about a book I was writing. I was gestured towards the Guardroom and went across to the side window with which I had grown familiar during the eight weeks before 30 June. It was an odd feeling, knowing my way about but not able to wander, for instance, over to the NAAFI for a mug of tea; and, strangest of all, not a red hackle in sight.

I was not sanguine because the current, published PLA policy, for the time being at least, was no access of any sort for the western press. However, armed with a letter from the Chief Executive – 'I would suggest you contact them [the PLA] direct regarding your intended visit' – and the friendly encounters between PLA and Black Watch I felt I should, at least, try to make post-handover contact.

I had gone without briefcase or camera, carrying only a large envelope of photographs, most of which are in this book. The PLA soldier at the window spoke some English and between us we seemed to make some sort of sense, especially when I produced one or two photos to catch his eye. Anyway, I was ushered into the Guardroom, offered a chair and invited to spread out the pictures whilst they rang for someone slightly more fluent.

An interpreter Captain duly arrived and there followed, for me, a fascinating conversation, the first of three, which lasted for over an hour. People kept drifting in and out and I suppose I talked to about a dozen officers during that time, covering a wide range of topics. Unsurprisingly, I found them all very courteous, interested in what I had to say and with a ready wit. The talk usually followed what was triggered off by particular photographs; the Jocks tidying up the cemetery drew approving comments, as did some of the final (wet) parade, the high-speed pursuit in rigid-hulled inflatable boats, the Friday morning Guard Ceremony at Prince of Wales Barracks; also various rest and recreation pictures, the Cenotaph, practising for the Dragon Boat Races – they said they were very keen to take part – the Hong Kong Sevens and the Black Watch Commanding Officer. 'A very kind man,' said the interpreter, who had met him and been to the Black Watch Stonecutters' Island Mess, 'a good man' and he tapped the photograph emphatically.

They were even more delighted by a picture of the large dragon that had been erected beside the Kowloon Star Ferry, an evening photo, and one of their first trucks arriving at the Prince of Wales Barrack gates early on the morning of 1 July. 'Very good picture,' they agreed with broad smiles.

Lieutenant Colonel Alasdair Loudon Commanding Officer, 1st Battalion, The Black Watch (RHR), Hong Kong, 1997.

(Frank Proctor)

I asked them if they knew that a lot of people had been very frightened and had thought they might come crashing over the border like Mongol hordes to sweep us all into the South China Sea. Again smiles, but serious this time, and nods; 'Tiananmen Square ... everybody thinks of Tiananmen Square ...' Then further discussion and less serious chat about food, and I told the story about the Jock, during a previous Black Watch tour, who had confided at Kai Tak Airport that he was glad to be going home, because Fife was the only place where you could get decent Chinese food.

I then switched to this book and told the Captain I was very anxious to balance the photographs, especially the off-duty or non-military ones, between the Black Watch and the PLA and wondered if it would be possible to come and chat to some of them and take casual photographs. He wrote it all down and said he would ask his General and would let me know. He hoped it would be possible but was not sure. Unfortunately, it did not work out, although they did send me a very pleasant message just before my departure for the UK. I remember thinking that I had been talking, to twist Deng Xiaoping's famous phrase, to 'Jocks with Chinese characteristics'.

I reminded them that, as far as I could work it out, the last time the Black Watch and the PLA had met was at the two battles of the Hook, in Korea, in November 1952 and told them that Colonel David Rose, the commanding officer, had said how very brave the Chinese were. I quoted his comment: 'The fortitude of the Chinese, in the face of our complete domination with all weapons, was truly staggering.' More nods, gleams in eyes, coughs. 'Thank you.'

I then asked a very good-looking PLA lieutenant what his unit was like and what he would like it to be. After making several points, he picked up a photograph of a Black Watch Guard striding jauntily behind a Piper: 'Like that,' he said with a most engaging smile.

The PLA Lieutenant's choice. Black Watch Guard marches on parade at Prince of Wales Barracks, Hong Kong. (Frank Proctor)

ENVOI

Hong Kong – S.A.R.

The new Special Administrative Region got off to a rocky start. Exceptionally heavy rain caused landslip and havoc, and newspapers were full of stories of children separated from parents as a result of illegal entry into Hong Kong. The legitimacy of the Provisional Legislature itself was challenged in the courts. Finally, three Court of Appeal judges ruled it a valid law-making body and most of Hong Kong breathed a collective sigh of relief. An attempt to invalidate the judicial system failed and the Solicitor-General, Daniel Fung, said the ruling 'clearly settles many of the controversies which have plagued the inception of the SAR'.

At the beginning of August, Typhoon Victor struck. A few weeks earlier and there would have been no farewell military parade. With the strongest winds for 14 years, the posting of a no.9 signal was the highest since 1983. Streets emptied as people hurried home to barricade doors and windows, the new Lantau Link was closed and at Kai Tak Airport passengers were stranded, as 250 departures and arrivals were delayed, cancelled or diverted. The MTR shut its overland routes and KCR trains stopped running. Forty-one people were injured across the territory and 279 were housed in shelters. A man died trying to rescue two men swept into the sea off Stanley Main Street.

However, the feared no. 10 signal heralding hurricane force winds, which had been forecast, was not needed. Inexplicably, as the eye of the storm swept over the Tsing Ma Bridge and moved further north across the New Territories it lost speed and was downgraded to a severe tropical storm.

On the cultural front there were concerts, events and exhibitions to celebrate Reunification. We enjoyed 'The Love For Our Motherland', a concert given by the Hong Kong City Chinese Orchestra, hearing amongst others Ching Sai-Wing on the erhu – the two-stringed fiddle of the Han Chinese, played like a 'cello – and Ng Hiu-Hung on the guzheng – which looks like a zither and is plucked.

The Chairman of the Hong Kong Artists' Association was not optimistic. In his introduction to 'Reunion and Vision', an art exhibition held in the Cultural Centre, Kowloon, he wrote:

> Apart from the smooth transition in political and economic aspects in the field of art and culture we do not see any new hope yet. The colonial multicultural mentality still haunts the territory.

Seven police officers were arrested in connection with a 'bribes for jobs' racket and police promotion boards tainted by investigation were scrapped. One thousand constables had to be reinterviewed by newly-appointed boards. The first batch of promotions, due in February, was expected to be delayed until May 1998.

Along the border with mainland China, three divisional police stations are to be upgraded to increase capacity following the restructuring of border policing. By October 1998 one of the present rotational 680-strong Field Patrol Detachment units, consisting of Police Tactical Unit officers, was to be amalgamated with the Border District Force, doubling its strength to 1,300. Thus efficiency is improved and the battle to stop a flood of illegal immigrants is intensified.

The prospect of elections in May 1998 – the first in the SAR – generated much speculation and some anxiety. Concern centred on a reduction in the size of the electorate for functional constituencies and a possible raising of the ceiling of funding for candidates in the geographical constituencies, the fear in the latter case being that politicians linked with big companies in Beijing would benefit. The Stock Exchange weathered serious financial storms, and chicken 'flu generated a re-think of hygiene regulations.

On 8 October 1997, the new Chief Executive, Tung Chee Hwa, rose at 6am and headed straight to his office in the Asia Pacific Finance Tower. Spending a final four hours working on his policy address, he then broke his habit of lunching alone in his office and dined at home on chicken and mushrooms with young bean sprouts and rice. He had not been expected to mix with the people as Governor Patten had and so had surprised many in his first days with his street-chat sessions, appearing in shirt sleeves. He had also decided not to move into Government House, with its British associations, rather to the initial dismay of the other residents in his block of flats, who feared the inevitable heavy security presence.

In his address the Chief Executive emphasised the vital need to improve the quality of the environment, not only in the city centre but in rural villages, country parks and the harbour. The new Administration would aim at 70 per cent home ownership by 2007 and strict measures would be adopted to curb excessive speculation. There were policy moves to help the old, the disabled and 'newly arrived citizens'. A sound regulatory system would lay a solid foundation for the further development of traditional Chinese medicine.

The Chief Executive urged the UK to discharge its continuing moral responsibility to assist in reaching a full solution to the refugee problem. Thirteen hundred refugees still remain in Hong Kong.

The Address got a mixed reception: 'He spent no more than 23 seconds and 83 characters on his guarantee for freedom of the press,' wrote Andy Ho in the *South China Morning Post*. 'Except for one sentence on press freedom there has not been one word about human rights,' said Emily Lau.

Martin Lee voiced disappointment at the Chief Executive's failure to stress freedom in his speech and, outside the Provisional Legislature, Democrats protested at the notion of imported labour. Citizens Party

Chairman, Christine Loh, commented that the Address had failed to stimulate political development and point the community in the right direction to achieve universal suffrage after 2007.

The Liberal Party Chairman, Alan Lee, on the other hand, welcomed the statement, saying it addressed many social problems overlooked by the Patten administration. 'We are happy because it has not politicised Hong Kong any more and shifts the focus to many pressing social problems.'

There does seem to be widespread belief that the Chief Executive is genuine in his concern for the environment and, indeed, other social concerns such as housing and education. But the question remains, for some, whether his administration realises how much has to be done and how little time there is.

So far, according to contacts in Hong Kong and elsewhere, Chinese pragmatism is winning the day and the SAR is progressing quietly and effectively. 'Pragmatism's the thing ... it's not a time for ideologies,' said a distinguished Sinologist. 'The Chinese are operating in the top section of the scale of possibilities.
Not off the scale because they've done *exactly* what was agreed, which is what they do.'

It would, for instance, have been conventional for the relevant Chinese ambassador to be present when the Chief Executive visits another country – the USA, Singapore, the UK. But, remarkably, apparently, Beijing has said 'we don't need to be there ... waste of time ... you get on with it.'

During the Stock Market fall, there were strong rumours that China was about to re-jig the currency, and Tung Chee Hwa wrote urgently reminding Beijing that such a move could make life very difficult for Hong Kong. He was speedily assured that the vulnerability of the Hong Kong economy was well understood and there were absolutely no plans for monetary change. 'That was good ... very good. Bodes well for the future,' was one comment; and another: 'This "you must stand up to the Chinese" nonsense is not the sort of thing they respond to at all. You must think ahead – now if we do this, they'll do that, then we'll have to do this and they'll have to do that etc.'

'There weren't enough chess players on our side towards the end.'

And the future? There's a greater determination to plan long-term, to think ahead – even 20 years. This is a marked difference from the recent past when the British administration got tied up in political wrangling and other matters got pushed aside. 'I hope that now the British have gone,' said a member of the SAR Executive Council, 'Hong Kong will soon have a better reputation in China, and will be much more empowered on the Mainland.'

WO1 Garrison Sergeant Major Vince Bell is now a reluctant civilian working in London. He misses his beloved Coldstream Guards and is worried about his future career. Nonetheless, he is resolutely trying to open new doors. He is very proud of the Gold Medal given to him by the PLA for his work with them up to the handover, which glitters on his beautiful sideboard from Bali.

When HMY *Britannia* and her escorts finally edged out from East Tamar and got underway, early on 1 July 1997, many people – who have since written about it – drove their cars all down the east side of Hong Kong Island trying to keep up with the illuminated flotilla, tears streaming down their faces.

On board HMS *Chatham*, Major General Bryan Dutton CB, CBE – the last British commander of the Hong Kong Garrison – thought over the last months. He was not to know but may have guessed that the PLA, a year on, would have an exemplary record. Later, he sent a telegram to the Black Watch and the other services and, at the end of his military career, found a quiet corner and stood alone for a while.

Three connected events:

Wang Dan, the former Tiananmen Square student leader was released from a long jail term on 19 April 1998 and flown to the US. His mother, Wang Lingyun, praised the early years of the PRC when, she said, the country had been moving in the right direction. She hopes there will now be improvements to people's basic rights to parallel the improvements in their living standards.

The appointment, in March 1998, of Zhu Rongji, who is highly

Congratulatory telegram to The Black Watch from Major-General Dutton. CB. CBE. July 1997.

regarded not only in China, but in the West, as Prime Minister, is interesting in this context, as he supports gradual political reform.

Mr Francis Cornish CHG, LVO–British Consul-General in Hong Kong–said on 14 November 1997 that Chief Executive Tung Chee Hwa has already persuaded the Chinese leadership that Hong Kong is in trustworthy hands and that his vision is leading 'quite easily' to consensus with China. He firmly believes that if Hong Kong expects 'two systems' to work, it must convince China that it believes in 'one country' and therefore sees itself as part of China.

Black Watch

In the December 1997 edition of the *Red Hackle* – the Black Watch magazine – B. Company notes:

The last day (30 June) was unavoidably drawn out and drama struck when a Lance Corporal fell down a monsoon drain whilst area cleaning and severely damaged his back. Sergeant Beattie (the medical sergeant) looked after him fantastically well but he could not be moved to hospital for fear of being left behind. (This is not allowed.) After a horrendous day and a very long journey home, he was despatched to hospital and has thankfully made a full recovery.

On 30 June 1997, one of the Jocks on final Border Guard duty who hauled down his O P's Union Jack at the end, was presented with it as a memento. On his return to the UK, he was swiftly offered £500 for it. He refused and, after more offers, auctioned it for a larger sum, the whole of which he donated to charity.

Visitors to the Black Watch Regimental Museum at Balhousie Castle, Perth, can see a dramatic painting of the battle of Quatre Bras (Chap. 4) entitled 'The Black Watch at Bay'. Colonel R T T Gurdon, until recently the regimental secretary, now says he has been able, after some impressive detective work, to identify the officer in the foreground of the picture, who is brandishing his claymore in exhortation.

On 24 August 1997, Captain Richard Haw MC, my company second-in-command in Berlin, died. A man of many parts – historian, naturalist, countryman, soldier, family man – the citation for his MC won in Korea, at the Hook, deserves partial repetition.

On the night of the 12 November 1952, Lieutenant Haw took a patrol to find enemy diggings on the 'Warsaw' feature. He made a full and

detailed reconnaissance which enabled him to lead a combined infantry and engineer demolition patrol the following night. This large group bumped the enemy on the way out, but got to its objective and proceeded to work. While the demolition charges were being laid, they were challenged in Chinese.

Lieutenant Haw, with commendable calmness and presence of

mind, replied to the challenge in a suitable tone (Urdu) and continued with the work till the job was completed at the approach of dawn.

On the night of the 18/19 November, during the attack on the Hook, he again showed good judgement and outstanding courage. When waiting to be called forward for a counter-attack, he and his men were under persistent shell- and mortar-fire. By his example and with complete disregard for his personal safety, he kept his men in high spirits under the most adverse conditions. When given orders to move forward for the final counter-attack and to clear the Hook at all costs, Lieutenant Haw, without hesitation, led his men through heavy shell-fire and methodically cleared the communication trenches ... His counter-attack task completed, he looked for something more to do. Despite the fact that the 'Warsaw' feature was still in enemy hands and several LMGs were still active in that area, Lieutenant Haw walked boldly out under fire with a small patrol and brought in three wounded who had been lying there throughout the night.

Rehearsing at Wellington Barracks, London (8 December 1997) for the Black Watch Pipes and Drums and the Band of the Scots Guards' US tour, Pipe Major Stephen Small said, with a smile that, yes, he had had a long wait in the rain to find out if his pipes were all right. He had done everything possible to prepare so could do no more except wait. The crowd must have wondered, he added, why there was such a long pause before his solo. This was, he went on to explain, because the television cameras wanted to watch the flags being folded. He had not thought at the time about the millions of viewers but had just concentrated on playing. Meanwhile there will be other jobs, not so historic, but just as satisfying. He does not see it as his biggest moment – yet. 'Perhaps ... when I look back,' he added.

Timothy Ainslie, BEM—wounded at Tobruk (chap. 4) with the 2nd Bn. Black Watch—trained him. He had gone as a spectator and got hooked. Timothy Ainslie, he said, taught more than the pipes, he fascinated you with glimpses of history and experience. 'He built character . . . he taught you how to behave.'

Second lieutenants Angus Philp and Piers Rennie were awarded the Swords of Honour at Sandhurst in April and August 1997. This means the Black Watch has more officers awarded this distinction being commissioned into the regiment than any other single battalion regiment. The former subaltern had the honour of posing with Her Majesty The Queen Mother, at the Fort George celebrations for her sixtieth year as Colonel-in-Chief, as Her Majesty's newest officer.

Back at Fort George, Inverness, WO2 CSM Gilfillan – Parade Colour Escort – confided it had been 'a tough tour ... very tough ... the toughest. It was the corporals and below who had it worst – non-stop hard work. They did very well.' It was good to be home, he added. Nine months in Kenya and Hong Kong were too long. That was the awful thing about

June 30 1997. Farewell Parade, Pipe Major Stephen Small.

(JSPRS)

247

being away – the separation from friends and family. Everybody begins to get fed up.

On Monday 8 September 1997, a Wessex helicopter of The Queen's Flight touched down at 1145 hrs, exactly as planned, on the northern rampart of Fort George, Inverness. Her Majesty Queen Elizabeth the Queen Mother had come to celebrate 60 years as Colonel-in-Chief with her former Commanding Officers (including Colonel David Rose DSO) and all those currently serving in the 1st Battalion. Her Majesty had never visited Fort George before and requested a pre-lunch tour. After this exploration and brief rest she had a private view of paintings commissioned to mark the presentation of New Colours at Birkhall in 1996 and then attended a small reception in a marquee on the south lawn to meet members of the Officers', Warrant Officers' and Sergeants' messes.

She responded to a Loyal Toast proposed by the colonel of the regiment, by saying how proud she was to have been Colonel-in-Chief for the past 60 years and how delightful it was to be with them, at home, in Fort George. Then, at precisely 1430 hrs, Her Majesty left the luncheon party and, with the Colonel of the Regiment and the Commanding Officer, visited a series of small displays mounted by the Companies, meeting families *en route*. It was a memorable visit for her regiment and all ranks look forward keenly to the next one.

Visiting Fort George on our return to the UK, we found the Adjutant, Ed Jones, still trying to deal with umpteen matters simultaneously but still finding time to advise and facilitate. He says he's recovered from Hong Kong.

HM The Queen Mother celebrates 60 years as Black Watch Colonel in Chief with her Regimental Sergeant Major – WO1 Alan McEwan – and other Warrant Officers at Fort George, Inverness. The Colonel of the Regiment – Brigadier G C Barnett, OBE – stands at her right hand. (Frank Proctor)

249

BIBLIOGRAPHY

Bartlett, M., *Over Hong Kong*. Odyssey Productions Ltd. (Hong Kong, 1990)

Bonavia, D., *Hong Kong 1997: The Final Settlement*. Columbus Books (1985)

Chang, J., *Wild Swans: Three Daughters of China*. HarperCollins (1991)

China Quarterly. Special Military Edition. (June 1996)

Cool, C., *The Lion and the Dragon*. Elm Tree Books (1985)

Cradock, P., *Experiences of China*. John Murray (1994)

David, S., *Churchill's Sacrifice of the Highland Division*. Brassey's (1994)

Evans, R, *Deng Xiaoping and the making of modern China*. Hamish Hamilton (1993)

Ferguson, T., *Desperate Siege: The Battle of Hong Kong*. Nelson Canada Ltd. (1980)

Fergusson, B., *Wavell: Portrait of a Soldier*. Collins (1950)

Fraser, G. M., *The General Danced at Dawn*. Fontana (1970)

Hastings, M., *The Korean War*. Michael Joseph (1987)

Hill, J., *A Bend in the Yellow River*. Phoenix House (1997)

Howard, P., *The Black Watch: Regimental Histories*. Hamilton (1968)

Jarvis, A, & Leng, C, *Hong Kong : A Society in Transition*. Routledge (1969)

Jay, A., *Elizabeth R.: The Role of Monarchy Today*. BBC Books (1992)

Jenner, W., *The Tyranny of History: The Roots of China's Crisis*. Penguin (1994)

Lewin, R., *The Chief: Field Marshal Lord Wavell*. Hutchinson (1980)

Linklater, E. & A., *The Black Watch*. Barrie & Jenkins (1961)

Lomax, E., *The Railway Man*. Jonathan Cape (1995)

Lu, L., *Li Lu: Moving the Mountain*. Macmillan (1990)

Napier, P., *Barbarian Eye. Lord Napier in China*. Brassey's (1995)

Parker, D., *A Brush with Hong Kong*. Odyssey Productions Ltd. (Hong Kong, 1990)

Patrikeef, F., *Mouldering Pearl. Hong Kong at the Crossroads*. George Phillip (1989)

Rose, D., *Off the Record: The Life and Letters of a BW Officer*. Spellmount (1996)

Segrave, S., *The Soong Dynasty*. Macmillan (1985)

Sinclair, D., *Queen and Country. The Life of Elizabeth the Queen Mother*. J.M. Dewi & Sons Ltd. (1979)

Stokes, E., *Hong Kong's Wild Places. An environmental explanation*. OUP (1995)

Suyin, H., *Wind in my Sleeve*. Jonathan Cape (1996)

Thomas, T. & Turner, N., *What's Going to Happen in 1997 in Hong Kong?* Corporate Communications Ltd. (1997)

Tim Keung, K. & Wordie, J., *The Ruins of War: A Guide to Hong Kong's Battlefields and Wartime Sites*. Joint Publishing (HK) Co. Ltd. (1996)

Wignall, S., *Spy on the Roof of the World*. Canongate (1996)

Yahuda, M., *Hong Kong: China's Challenge*. Routledge (1996)